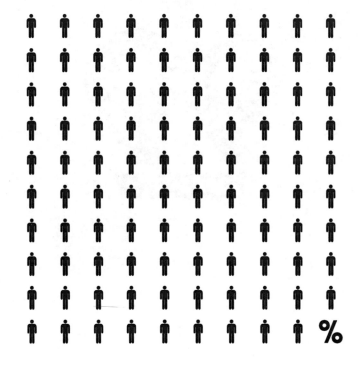

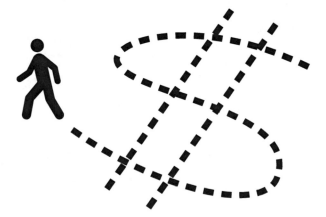

99 NIGHTS WITH THE

99

PERCENT

Dispatches from the First Three Months of the Occupy Revolution

CHRIS FARAONE

THIS IS A WRITE TO POWER PRODUCTION

Cover and Book Design by: Alfredo C. Rico-Dimas
Cover Photo by: Derek Kouyoumjian

The author gratefully acknowledges the help and support of *The Boston Phoenix*, in which portions of this book have appeared.

ISBN 978-0-9851059-0-7

Web: Facebook.com/OccupyBook
Email: mail@writetopower.net

Printed in the USA

JUN 2 9 2012

The Dirty Version

In Memory Of...

Jamie Hall

Clif Garboden

Carole Belmonte

DEDICATION

This book is for anyone who's starved in a First World country, and for anybody who has ever had to sleep outside of a building in which million-dollar condos sit empty. It's for the families whose lives were demolished by the modern architects of inequity, and to those who were forced onto the street by bankers who would rather horde vacant properties than provide shelter.

My work is for everyone who makes pizzas or lays bricks for a living, and for those who believe that laborers are more important than stock brokers. It's for all the people who called the police on me when I was just trying to make some money, and also for pot bellied finance chumps, because without them there'd be no class warfare.

Everything that's happened so far with Occupy proves that change is possible, and that artists, working stiffs, and even middle-class folks can unite against the bastards who robbed us all and left the world holding the bag. This project, and these articles, were written with all of those 99 percenters in mind, and with a heart full of hope from watching them finally stand up for themselves.

- Chris Faraone, January 17, 2012

CONTENTS

99 NIGHTS WITH THE 99 PERCENT

I remember the exact moment when I heard that the Occupy bug bit Boston. I was on an Orange Line platform in Roxbury, moving toward an escalator that I ride when I'm too hungover to climb stairs. It was mid-afternoon in that time of the year with cold mornings but warm days, so I'd removed my sweat-soaked Sox hat and green hoodie and was affixing the latter to my backpack. An older African-American woman with a wire pushcart full of bagged groceries – who I'd met a week earlier at a foreclosure eviction blockade in Dorchester – waved a copy of the *Boston Metro* in my face.

"Did you see this?" she yelled. "Occupy Wall Street is coming here. They're coming to shame our banks too!"

Word from the street to the tweet was that the first Occupy Boston general assembly was planned for that night of September 27, 2011. I'd been fascinated with the movement – consuming as many articles and blog posts as possible about the Wall Street actions – but it hadn't dawned on me that Boston would be next. Chicago activists had convened in the name of Occupy days earlier, but operational problems persisted, and a notion prevailed that an encampment was unlikely to blossom there under the watch of Mayor Rahm Emmanuel and his newly minted municipal machine.

Since my job is to report on oppressed peoples – a demographic that's been growing rapidly for some time – I wasn't totally surprised by the development. The past year had been hectic, with more protests and public aggravation than I'd ever witnessed on my beat. Folks were swarming public spaces to defend their jobs. Communities were mobilizing against Walmart. In the weeks right before Occupy erupted, I'd become particularly privy to the nightmare of foreclosures, having tailed activists to a number of anti-bank actions from Dorchester to the suburbs.

Psychologists would call my recollection of hearing about Occupy a "flashbulb memory" – either that or post-traumatic stress disorder. The flashbulb phenomenon is typically used to describe occasions that impact people so profoundly that they remember details with photographic specificity: what shoes they were wearing, their mood, who they were toasting cocktails with. In my lifetime, the most stand-out examples are probably the day when the Challenger exploded, and that awful morning in September. Most people who lived through those calamities know what color underwear they crapped when the news reached them.

My first reaction to getting scooped was to skip my daily walk to work, jump in a taxi, and speed into the office to blast Occupy organizers for failing to float me a press release. In fact I stepped even further, gassing the entire movement, in a blog post, for its hostility toward reporters. I'd been obsessed with the taking of Zuccotti Park, but had also grown frustrated with the running Occupy line about a so-called "media blackout." I've seen blackouts – in fact, at the time, thousands of Verizon workers were marching daily with little to no coverage. Occupy Wall Street, contrarily, got attention from major outlets ranging from

Fox and CNN to Bloomberg and *The Week* – all before the first blast of pepper spray.

Not that anything could have stopped me from covering them. I agreed with virtually everything that Occupy was throwing at the Wall – wealth disparity is out of hand, corporate lobbyists are crooked, those who plundered the financial system should be jailed or worse. With that in mind, I became compelled to look under the hood and get inside of tents not just in Boston and New York, but wherever the energy spread and my sock drawer bank account could get me. It was a no-brainer; I'd spent most of my adult life giving a voice to those who suffer at the hands of plutocrats. Now they had a banner – "The 99 Percent" – and a home base in my backyard.

I've no clue what I'd be doing if the movement never happened. Not long before my life became occupied, I'd backed out of a long-term relationship, and convinced myself that fate must have cleared my schedule so I could work around the clock. In the last three months of 2011, catch-up calls with friends were limited to seconds, and I didn't see close relatives at all, except for some in Queens who I stayed with when the concrete at Zuccotti was too cold to nap on. I even compromised my side career as a music critic, as at least a dozen micro-genres have buzzed and flamed out since I last gave a fuck.

But through the whole hustle – after setting my alarm for every hour on some nights to check if camps had been raided – I was able to witness a cultural shift that hardly registered in most media coverage. Occupiers had exaggerated their cries of a "blackout," but the quality of reporting, as they also alleged, was mostly piss poor. Television journalists, their faces dusted with goo and blush, were reluctant to muddy their shoes in the camps. As for reliable lefty outlets; plenty of sites and publications put boots on the ground, but too often it was to gush over the Manhattan action, with countless writers chronicling "how it all started" and, after the flagship camp was raided, "what the future holds for the movement." I'm glad that there are numerous oral histories and however many Occu-mentaries in production, but my goal from the get-go was to hit this from a different angle – to watch Occupy take its first steps outside of New York. It was a magic carpet ride through an exhilarating tear gas gauntlet, and to be honest, I wasn't too concerned about how it all started or when it might end.

ON THE MAP

Activists took Dewey Square in Boston on September 30. I wasn't there on account of a trip I'd planned to see my mom in Florida. While I always love relaxing visits to her "active adult" community, I'd have probably postponed my arrangements if not for the chance to see a beachfront revolution brew at Occupy Miami. I was sad to miss the inevitable drama that would pop in Boston, but the thought of the movement migrating down the coast intrigued me. To psych myself up I even had a romanticized image of Occupy Miami based on the detainee camp scene in *Scarface*, a fantasy filled with thousands of badass activists who don't break their balls, or their word, for no one.

Occupy Miami wasn't quite like I'd imagined, but the afternoon that I spent at their first-ever meeting opened my eyes wide. Watching folks who were thousands of miles from Zuccotti employ the same hand signals that were also used at Boston's kickoff assemblies on the Common – and hearing the same economic horror stories echoed from back home – I realized that Occupy was no flash in the pan. Nor was it some cheap franchise like the ministry of decrepit cult leader Lyndon LaRouche, whose minions attempted to peddle his anti-Semitic trash at Occupy camps everywhere until they were flushed out. Unlike the failed and fractured lefty movements that I'd covered in the past, this one appeared to have long legs.

Upon returning to Boston, I rode the airport express bus right to Dewey, bags still slung over my sunburnt shoulders. I emerged from the terminal at South Station with no clue what to expect; to my limited knowledge, a large group had rallied against cops near the Federal Reserve Bank days earlier, and in the time since had begun to build a small city. I hadn't realized the extent of their accomplishments; in a few days they'd erected more than 100 tents, and constructed full-service medical and food prep facilities.

After focusing on Occupy Boston for two days – and marching several times with protesters – it became clear that my hunch in Miami was spot-on. Occupy was fertile and agile, and so I would ride along like a storm chaser. A group called Stop the Machine planned to swarm Washington DC on October 6 to protest the invasion of Afghanistan a decade earlier. If this movement planned to address war and economic woes – those mischievous cousins who are rarely disciplined together – I wanted to be there. The year before, I'd covered Jon Stewart's "Rally to Restore Sanity" and Glenn Beck's "Restoring Honor" bash in DC, both of which were plenty entertaining. But it was refreshing to see a serious cause get some attention for a change.

Being in DC that week, and in Baltimore and Philly after that, I was wowed by the intense emotion and the sheer magnitude of Occupy enthusiasm. The movement had exploded, teetering on what seemed like the brink of control. In DC, a group of mostly college students had moved into McPherson Square, flown a banner, and set up a supply drop and food table. At the same time, Stop the Machine, which was camping on nearby Liberty Plaza, had also mounted the Occupy bandwagon, even telling participants to brand tweets with an #OccupyDC hashtag. The dueling occupations caused confusion and resentment; at one point when I was there, the young McPherson set even marched, drums blazing, through an anti-war speak-out, infuriating veterans and older activists.

In comparison, Occupy Baltimore was smaller, with a decidedly artsy flare. This was the place where I first realized how much difficulty Occupy would have attracting people of color, when a black passerby screamed at the sadistic spectacle before her of a white brunette – dressed in black heels and a chic red coat – pretend-choking a black male Occupier who "represented working people." The so-called "Military-Industrial-Complex S&M Pageant" alarmed the African-American pedestrian, who had come to enjoy one of the chain restaurants behind Baltimore's mall-side encampment, but wound up leaving with a foul taste in her mouth from the movement. In the weeks that followed, I'd see this kind of culture clash play out across the country.

After my brain cells were battered by non-stop overnight drum circles at Occupy Philly, I headed at last to the New York mothership. There I found the root of every Occupation that I'd been to: Zuccotti's flamboyant anarchists, with their onyx nail polish and street theater, reminded me of Baltimore's contingent; likewise, the chaos and perpetual percussion made Wall Street sing just like Philly. Camp-wise, Zuccotti – though still tent-less at the time – had many of the same amenities as its satellite in Boston, from a working library to a meditation zone to over-educated media reps and grub handled by Food Not Bombs. The corporations that Occupy abhors spend inordinate amounts of time and money expanding and marketing their empires across state lines. This operation took less than three weeks to multiply and clone itself from coast to coast.

BOOM TOWN

The full weight of Occupy smacked me square across the face in Seattle, not long after the dankest mushrooms that I've ever feasted on kick-flipped through my stomach. I was hanging with two seasoned hackers from the Web activist group Anonymous, learning about their complex system of scanning cop frequencies in every city where police threats loomed large. Before we could finish, though, a print reporter who I'd met earlier walked up and stole me away to ask if I had a rag. I didn't, so he passed me a towel and told me to toss it in a bucket full of vinegar and orange juice. In the event that I got peppered, I was instructed to scrub my eyes with the rinse.

I'd headed west to examine the toll that police violence was taking on the movement. And in Seattle, the sentiments of fellow reporters gave me a sense that free speech was being quashed, as did an incident there the day before, when an 85-year-old woman had her wrinkles filled with pepper spray during a post-march fiasco. Due to the national outrage and negative attention that ensued, the prevailing notion was that Seattle cops would likely take it easy for the few days that coincided with my being there. Still, I was reminded that journalists sometimes get hit first, and the thought of getting sprayed while tripping freaked me out.

That's when the doors of Seattle Central Community College – which hosted Occupiers on its campus – swung open. More than 100 students rushed out onto the landing. They stomped past tents towards the street, now with hundreds more in tow behind them. I know I was a hallucinating tourist, but it felt like everyone had marching orders except me. It was raining hard, and I was the only one distracted by the downpour. I wasn't prepared either. Most people were sporting slickers, plastic bags, and even goggles – trusty shields against both Pacific Northwest weather and spicy projectiles. I had on jeans and a windbreaker, both of which were fully soaked just minutes into the five-hour action.

By the time the bandana-clad activists finished swinging from the University of Washington bridge – scolding campus Republicans for blocking school solidarity with Occupy – I needed more than a few drinks to balance the mushrooms I'd been munching since breakfast. As arranged, I scooped a resident camp hero named Chris at the medic tent, where he'd earlier shown me the beet-red chemical burns that he'd endured in clashes with police. Chris is a tall but fit homeless National Guard veteran and trained emergency responder whose leg was crushed in Baghdad when a building landed on him. After returning home, mobile but disabled, he mostly slept under bridges and on couches until Occupy started.

Chris is a 99 Percent poster boy. As in tune with policy as any armchair wonk I met along the way, he had big plans for how to push Occupy forward. Specifically, he was raising money for a bus for Seattle medics to steer on long marches, and maybe even bring to other cities. He's tough, having learned to scrap for everything since early on; but he's also non-threatening, a gentleman Bud Light drinker who offered me his last smoke (until he opened up his pack and realized it was empty). Chris grew up underground, and has ridden boxcars through more towns than most people have ever heard about. And when given the opportunity, he enlisted in the military, and enthusiastically deployed to Iraq.

Me and Chris got loose, smoking joints and slugging beers until four in the morning. At that point I had to break out and phone-in a talk radio interview with an amenable conservative back in Boston, where it was three hours later. With the tail end of my trip shining through a fog of booze and weed, nudging me toward higher consciousness, the chat turned out to be enlightening as I was accused – not for the first time – of thinking everyone should have a *Town & Country* dream home and two new cars. That was the popular right-wing claim to link Occupy and socialism; all disenfranchised folks, liberals allegedly believe, yearn for a government-subsidized life of luxury.

It took hundreds of conversations with Occupiers like Chris – and prodding from some conservative gasbags – before I finally realized what's behind that mentality of Occupy adversaries. They're actually correct about one thing – Occupiers, along with anybody else who's cheering for change, really do have an ideal vision for how things should be. But what a lot of people don't get is that the Occupy dream, at least as I understand it, hardly resembles the grotesquely gilded fantasies that most one-percenter wannabees masturbate to. Not a single person who I met in any camp expressed hopes for handouts before hopes for jobs, let alone believed that anybody owed them a McMansion and a WaveRunner.

Things changed soon after I returned from the West Coast, where I also hit the militarized likes of Portland, as well as Occupy San Francisco and Oakland, where I saw Black Panther legacies march side-by-side with union toughs and software developers. Within a few weeks, it seemed like camps were being raided everywhere – battles in Los Angeles, showdowns in Denver, brutality in Texas. Guys like Chris, who joined the movement to defend human rights like fair wages and affordable healthcare, were forced into constant defense mode.

When Dewey Square got raided in the early hours of December 10 – nearly three months after the Wall Street action started – I stood among writers, Ivy Leaguers, homeless teens, steelworkers, transsexuals, hipsters, hippies, professionals, professors, and all sorts of other characters. Despite having been awake for days, I remember the looks on all of their faces. Some wept as their camp was crushed; others screamed as their friends were stuffed into meat wagons. It was major news; Zuccotti had been stormed a month earlier, and Dewey was the movement's longest-running camp in a major city. As I stood there, watching tents get bulldozed, someone behind me said that an era was getting loaded into a dump truck, never to be seen again. They might be right, but I'll have the flashbulb memories forever.

September 17 | Day 1

Adbusters called them
To bring message to bastards
Occupy Wall Street

September 18 | Day 2

Troopers want to camp
Robot cops say can't crash there
No tents no problem

September 19 | Day 3

Current TV comes
Olbermann to the rescue
Mister Occupy

September 20 | Day 4

Police say no masks
And even make some arrests
No clue what's to come

September 21 | Day 5

Troy Davis murdered
Savannah shows no mercy
Occupy responds

September 22 | Day 6

Black New York reacts
Thousands head to Union Square
In name of Davis

September 23 | Day 7

Zuccotti renamed
Swarm calls it Liberty Square
Their park from now on

September 24 | Day 8

Mass march no permit
Mad arrests and pepper spray
Rogue cop caught on tape

September 25 | Day 9

Chicago acts up
Anons threaten New York cops
Nation now watching

September 26 | Day 10

Meathead is revealed
Who peppered woman on march
Tony Baloney

DO THE FIGHT THING

Originally published in:
The Boston Phoenix, August 10, 2011

I often say that my colleague David Bernstein covers politics, while I cover how politics affect people. That job description doesn't completely make sense as much as it makes for a good sound bite, since we both report on plenty of political theater, as well as on the real-life repercussions of legislative stupidity. But for a while now I've particularly focused on people who are pissed off at politicians, and on citizens who are worried about everything from unemployment to civil rights. While I've done several protest round-ups through the years, by the time "Do the Fight Thing" came out – roughly a month before Occupy surfaced – the public seemed especially riled. Not everyone was crying economic woes, but it didn't take a sociologist to see that their problems stemmed from the financial mess that would soon unite folks everywhere.

Boston burned last week, with pandemonium blazing from Beacon Hill to Dorchester's foreclosed ghettos. Union flags were flown, loud music roared, and fleets of motorcycles rumbled, as several thousand people marched for civil rights and human dignity, and, in at least one case, to scold moguls for banking gross salaries at the expense of workers.

According to the Cambridge-based National Bureau of Economic Research, which determines when recessions start and end, the meltdown that began in 2007 cooled off last year. But despite that rosy reassurance, the unemployment rate has hovered at around nine percent for 28 months, and is showing no real sign of recovery. Just this past week, Wall Street suffered its biggest drop since the peak of economic wreckage three years ago.

To worsen matters, the recent debt-ceiling quagmire reminded Americans that they're governed by a callous brood of bozos. If there was ever faith – on the left or the right – that either Barack Obama or the Tea Party would steer us onto a more comfortable course, it's flown the way of the bald eagle.

Boston feels the pain. In addition to an awful rash of violence – 159 shootings and 34 homicides so far this year – vacant storefronts and suspended building projects add insult to tragedy. There have been small victories; last week, for example, the perpetual protest group City Life/Vida Urbana, along with more than 100 picketers, stalled an eviction on Normandy Street near Franklin Park. But this is a long war, with countless theaters and no apparent end. Here's a view from the front lines.

MINORITY MINORITY REPORT
Two weeks ago, the Urban League of Eastern Massachusetts hosted its national organization's annual conference in the Hub, generating much fanfare and a 42-page document titled The State of Black Boston. The report covered a gamut of critical issues,

from education and development to media and culture, but omitted at least one significant topic: blacks with disabilities, and their alarming unemployment rate.

With that snub in mind, last week, seasoned rally-goers from the Union of Minority Neighborhoods (UMN) joined disabled organizers on Beacon Street, where the unified front sparked an overdue dialogue about the welfare of Boston's most marginalized citizens. While the press turnout was abysmal, the crowd eventually grew to more than 40 people, with a few influential leaders – including South End state representative Byron Rushing – showing up to lend support. Animated activists like Toni Saunders, executive director of the Dudley Square–based Associated Advocacy Center, lured in passers-by with passionate pleas.

"Our children are dying," said Saunders. "They're being bullied and excluded, they're drugged, and in some cases, they're committing suicide." Florette Willis of the Roxbury mental-health advocacy group M-Power kicked it up a notch, comparing modern disability apartheid to the foulest institution of all: "Before I be a slave," she declared, "I be buried in my grave."

As tourists zipped by on Segways, Saunders, Willis, and half a dozen others dropped bombshells. They said that a disproportionate 37 percent of Boston residents with disabilities reside in communities of color like Dorchester and Mattapan. Furthermore, according to the 2009 American Community Survey (conducted by the US Census Bureau), only about 25 percent of black Bostonians with disabilities are employed. "The numbers are stunning," said Keith Jones, a tireless disabled-rights fighter who has cerebral palsy. "And those numbers aren't by happenstance."

This is a new beginning for their cause; facilitators claimed that in the face of their omission from the Urban League report, disabled minorities are more determined to be heard now than they've ever been before. "Wherever there's a discussion about the state of black Boston," said Willis of M-Power, "people with disabilities need to have a seat at that table."

WHAT THE FOX?

Rupert Murdoch's wet glove of a face was everywhere outside the State House last Thursday. Baking in a half-circle on the bricks beneath the Golden Dome, members of the Boston Media Reform Network (BMRN) shielded themselves from the sun with popsicle masks portraying the media magnate. They also carried signs stamped with slogans like "What the Fox?" – but it was the sea of wrinkly Murdoch visages that paused commuters in their tracks.

The group turned out about 50 people, from bespectacled young optimists, to seasoned demonstrators, to a few in between. Their demand: that congress and the Federal Communications Commission (FCC) investigate – and possibly yank licenses from – stateside media outlets owned by Murdoch's News Corporation, under legal fire in the UK for sleazy practices at its shamed *News of the World*.

Having hosted lead-up powwows to paint placards and rap strategy, BMRN facilitators Jason Pramas and Bill Hodges came rhetorically equipped for battle, soldiering through the taunting of a Murdoch-loving yuppie who suggested, from the sidelines, that they go home and "blog about it." Mary Alice Crim, an outreach manager from the Western Mass–based media-reform nonprofit Free Press, blasted Murdoch for contributing to a monopolistic media landscape in which "only a handful of companies control what we read."

Local NBC affiliate WHDH covered the spectacle, as did Murdoch's own Fox 25, which left before the colorful band of progressives crossed the street for their encore picket of the station's Beacon Hill outpost. It's too bad – the offensive was leagues more entertaining than when lone activists sit across Beacon Street during the morning newscast, only to have their placards blocked from the screen by commentator Doug "VB" Goudie's titanic ego.

The protest attracted more curiosity than spite; for the most part, onlookers chuckled at the Murdoch masks, and some fellow Fox-haters even propped the activists, who played the corner of Park and Beacon streets for 15 minutes before police asked them to chill. They obliged, but not before one last spat with a Fox legionnaire, this one a tucked-in armchair Hannity on vacation with his family, who screamed from his duck boat: "Get a job, you dirty hippies." Without hesitation, one protester in a Rasta beanie replied: "Quack quack, you fascist. Go back to wherever, so long as it's not here."

CAN YOU HEAR THEM NOW?
A blood-red swarm flooded Post Office Square last Thursday night: thousands of Verizon field workers and their allies, shouting demands in the shadows of their financial-service-industry oppressors. At the time, contracts for nearly 45,000 laborers – represented by the Communications Workers of America and International Brotherhood of Electrical Workers (IBEW) – were two days from expiring, forcing those people off the job until the telecom behemoth and its employees reached agreements on pensions, job security, and sick days.

(By press time, Verizon workers had gone on strike. They continue to refuse the company's demands for significant concessions, arguing that Verizon earned nearly $7 billion in profits so far this year, and crying foul about the hundreds of millions in compensation that top executives continue to take home.)

The Post Office Square showdown wasn't the week's first action relative to this cause. The day before, about 100 workers and civil-rights organizers gathered outside of another Verizon building – on Cambridge Street, near the Bowdoin T stop – to picket a related management proposal for eliminating Martin Luther King Jr.'s birthday as a paid holiday. But Thursday's grand-finale protest dwarfed all of the week's prior demonstrations. Held outside of the Franklin Street building that housed much of Verizon's local workforce until earlier this year, this one delivered a backdrop and theatrics to match the media attention.

"They're on the way with a coffin full of old contracts," Paul Feeney, legal director for the Local 2222 chapter of the IBEW, announced to the arriving crowd. Standing on a makeshift stage beside a riled roster of Massachusetts union stalwarts, Feeney took the first shot of the evening at Verizon fat cats. "Maybe," said Feeney, "by the end of the weekend, [Verizon president and CEO] Lowell McAdam will be in [that casket], too."

The music set the mood. As old friends mingled in the moment, waiting for more buses to arrive, Guns 'N Roses lit up the sound system, followed by Quiet Riot, Dropkick Murphys, and some requisite AC/DC fire-starters. It was the type of tough horde that knows how to fight – Rosie the Riveter and Lenny Clarke look-a-likes who whistle with their fingers and take shit from no one. Warned by their HR departments, many local businessmen steered clear of the scene, prudently avoiding angry rallygoers in SCAB HUNTER T-shirts.

As more than two dozen supporters rolled up on choppers, the massive inflatable union rat effigy beside the dais appeared to be actually smoking the cigar between his chompers. And then came the American flags, followed by the National Anthem and several screeds against Verizon's move to make employees work on MLK and Veterans Day. "They have some fucking audacity," said Bob Haynes, outgoing president of the commonwealth contingent of the AFL-CIO.

Though pols and bureaucrats often disappear in August, scores of officials rallied with the workers. City councilors Tito Jackson, Mike Ross, and John Connolly stood in the thick of all the action, as did community leaders like Reverend William Dickerson, of Dorchester's Greater Love Tabernacle, who served up some humor along with his spiritual guidance. "Can you hear me now?" asked Dickerson, rhetorically, referencing Verizon's eternally irksome advertising campaign.

In his turn defending "good, decent, dignified jobs," Massachusetts congressman Bill Keating harnessed the spirit, pulling a loose union tee down over his snug polo shirt. A rookie lawmaker in Washington, Keating expressed extreme dissatisfaction with inaction in the nation's capital, offering words that, while meant to hype the telecom crowd, summarized sentiments that have been brewing all throughout New England this summer, and that finally erupted in the streets last week.

"Working and middle-class people are under attack," said Keating, a former Norfolk County district attorney whose powerful podium poise fit right in with the bombast of his bullhorn-happy labor comrades. "[Congress] is just kicking the can down the road. Instead of finding solutions, they're kicking middle-class Americans down the road."

VIDA URBANA

Originally published in:
The Boston Phoenix, September 30, 2011

For years, I've known that City Life is at the national forefront of the war on foreclosures. Located blocks from my apartment in Jamaica Plain, the storied organization had discovered that, by working with local banks and credit unions – and shaming ruthless lenders by staging publicized eviction blockades – they could help keep families off the street. In years past I'd covered their unique actions, like when City Life artists projected silhouettes in the windows of vacant homes. (Think Kevin McCallister's stunt with the blow-up clown in *Home Alone 2*). But this time, along with labor and nonprofit federations Right to the City and MassUniting, they came to raise a heap of hell. Years from now, the history books will probably show that Occupy spurred people to fight foreclosures. This account acknowledges the simmering outrage that precipitated the mass movement for homeowner rights.

There are about 1500 pissed-off people lacing up their shitkickers around Boston right now. They're airbrushing placards, photocopying fliers, and in some cases preparing to be arrested. It's been more than three years since the nation's biggest banks pillaged the economy and screwed American homeowners, and these activists think it's time to quit taking it and start throwing haymakers.

More than a dozen orgs have united to mastermind a multilateral attack for the ages. For the progressive left, which can have a hard time getting its act together, this is a rare phenomenon. Like other urban centers that have been hit hard by the mortgage crisis, Boston has taken its knocks: roughly 7000 Massachusetts residents were put on eviction row in 2011, more than 1400 in July alone. But nowhere else have people been able to fight back against abusive banks in such a sustained or organized way.

The difference is that here, everyone is at the same table, and that table is a group called MassUniting. Formed in April by Democratic and progressive activists, they've managed to reach out to various groups and choreograph them into a cohesive front.

"We're bringing divergent groups together," says Jason Stephany, spokesperson for MassUniting. "People are hurting and looking for any way possible to change their situation, and we're trying to give them a productive way to do that."

In July, MassUniting coordinated a 400-person Dorchester speak-out. In August, they crashed Republican Senator Scott Brown's fundraiser with a brass band. Two weeks ago, female activists disguised themselves as servers and infiltrated a posh BoA breakfast at the Seaport Hotel. All summer, smaller groups of activists have picketed dozens of BoA branches, culminating in a delivery of a truckload of trash – collected from the unkempt yard of a foreclosed BoA property in Malden – to the doorstep of a Beacon Hill townhouse belonging to the bank's Massachusetts president, Robert Gallery.

These campaigns aren't just political theater. They get actual results. For example: the Jamaica Plain-based advocacy nonprofit City Life/Vida Urbana, a major player in MassUniting's coalition, has spent the last three years staging eviction blockades – arriving en masse the day foreclosed homes are to be auctioned off and physically disrupting the proceedings. That, along with other tactics, like counseling homeowners and negotiating on their behalf with banks, has helped keep more than 1000 families off the street.

Now, with the national umbrella org Right to the City hosting its annual convention in Boston this weekend, activists from across the country are parachuting in to join forces with their Boston brethren.

Their target: Bank of America's Federal Street offices. Their mission: to give BoA a swift kick in the balls.

"When you back people into a corner, they're going to fight back," says Stephany. "Trust me – this is just the opening salvo."

GATHERING FORCES
With 15 days to go before the planned BoA action downtown, Stephany and MassUniting director Angela DeLeo are greeting members of their small army in the South Bay Plaza parking lot.

They're gathered near the BoA branch building, and are easy to spot with their stacks of neon orange signs and fliers. About two dozen people mingle and discuss the day's offensive. Organizers say it should go down like recent operations in Grove Hall and Fields Corner, where MassUniting paraded around BoA branches shouting taglines like "BIG BANKS, YOU CAN'T HIDE – WE CAN SEE YOUR GREEDY SIDE" – before occupying the lobby.

Once inside, the swarm attracts both ire and attention. A few queued customers ignore the activists – fiddling with their smart phones and avoiding eye contact – but most people are receptive and take the literature. As DeLeo and others chant MassUniting's slogan du jour – "BANK OF AMERICA – BAD FOR AMERICA" – a manager finally notices them and heads in their direction. Nobody puts up a fight, and they all vacate after just five minutes, but not before taping their demands on bank windows and littering the counters with fact sheets listing BoA's abhorrent practices.

These are old lefty tactics from the '60s: civil disobedience, public disruption, mass rallies. Recently, though, you're more likely to see Tea Partiers utilizing these strategies.

"The Tea Party is kind of the right-wing version of us, or at least we're a counterweight to what they're doing," says Stephany. A former Wisconsin Democratic Party leader, the 28-year-old Stephany became a target for conservatives after MassUniting's "Bobblehead Brown" campaign, in which the group exposed gaps between the senator's labor rhetoric and his Wall Street-friendly voting record.

"The Tea Party went door to door, they went to churches, they went to NRA meetings, and they told people how to get things done," says Stephany. "We learned from that."

So it's ironic that, in stealing back liberal stunts, MassUniting has won the scorn of Tea Party poster boys like Brown, whose campaign tagged them as a "far-left front group for the Service Employees International Union." (That's part right; MassUniting is backed by the SEIU, among others.) They've also been painted with the same brush that libs often apply to the Tea Party. Rob Eno, a conservative blogger for Red Mass Group, has attacked MassUniting efforts as "astroturfing" – insinuating that it's a fake grassroots movement actually fueled by out-of-state funding and directed by national progressive entities. MassUniting says the only truth in that allegation is that Stephany recently moved from Wisconsin – but not as a national Democratic operative; he came to live with his girlfriend.

Over a span of two months this past spring, about 70 MassUniting workers and volunteers knocked on 70,000 doors across the commonwealth. By June, they'd signed up more than 14,000 potential soldiers. Which is how this posse wound up here, in South Bay Plaza, getting shooed away from the drive-thru teller area by bank management.

As they disperse into the parking lot, sliding their remaining fliers under windshield wipers, they chorus with conviction: "WE'LL BE BACK."

TENT REVIVAL
Every Tuesday, City Life hosts a "bank-tenant" meeting at its Amory Street war bunker. By 7pm there's over 100 people here, and the session is in full swing. As a first order of business, new recruits are sworn in. One woman drove in from Randolph, where her Sun Trust loan caved in, while another first-timer tells of a Freddie Mac loan that recently sank below sea level. To embolden them, newcomers are presented with an info packet and a three-foot wooden sword, the latter of which they're told to hoist like He-Man as they're asked if they're prepared to fight. Once they say "YES," the crowd responds loudly and in unison, "THEN WE'LL FIGHT WITH YOU."

There's only standing room left by the time they discuss the September 30 anti-BoA actions, which one regular calls, "the big bout that we've been waiting for." A City Life organizer, legendary activist Steve Meacham, lays out the game plan for the following week and asks for volunteers for specific missions. He also tells them what to expect – from police, passers-by, and their own cohorts.

Heavy boos erupt every time offending banks are named. BoA gets extra-loud shouts – following one mention, people holler "STAND UP FIGHT BACK" over and over for several minutes.

Toward the end, Meacham and other organizers lend a last bit of encouragement, asking the crowd, "How many times have you felt in your heart that thousands of people need to come out and fight together?" Meacham continues: "This extraordinary crisis requires extraordinary measures, because we're no longer in a skirmish. This is a battle, and this time we're on offense, so we have to push a little harder. Look at what they've done to us – now it's time to go to their homes and disrupt their lives."

ONE MAN'S TRASH ON ANOTHER MAN'S TREASURE

The next day, Meacham is standing on the northwest corner of the Public Garden sporting his trademark red baseball cap, blue button-down, and bullhorn. The City Life operatives around him are hard to miss in their bright green gear, as are their MassUniting comrades in their electric-orange T-shirts. This joint operation began days earlier, when people from both groups collected garbage from a foreclosed BoA property in Malden. After being told to leave the bank branch where they attempted to discard the trash, activists thought it fitting to drop the waste off at BoA president Gallery's Beacon Hill home.

The group is momentarily set back as one woman faints from the heat and excitement. After she's hauled off in an ambulance, a City Life point man yells "LET'S GET IT," and leads the flock of 30 toward the target. A young blonde on Gallery's stoop looks up from her cell phone and sees a swarm approaching her – carrying giant bags of rubbish and chanting "WE CAN'T TAKE IT ANY MORE – GONNA LEAVE THIS TRASH ON GALLERY'S DOOR."

She turns and locks herself in the house.

Mimicking the foreclosure papers that many of them have been served, today's team brought a "notice to quit" for Gallery, a giant copy of which they promptly affix to the executive's distinguished door with duct tape. It reads: "Please be advised that we represent middle-class and low-income families in Massachusetts – the citizens who have been most greatly affected by Bank of America's destructive business practices. You and your bank are hereby notified to quit the following activities within nine (9) days of this Notice."

As the group chants and seethes, people read the demands over a bullhorn – the most critical of which is that BoA "halt all foreclosures and evictions until underwater mortgages can be renegotiated." The nine-day notice expires this Friday – the day they plan to storm the downtown area. In the meantime, though, everybody's goal is to spread the word, and people seem to be listening. There's a steady stream of honks from passing drivers, while a tattooed tough from the city's Water and Sewer Commission stops his truck in the middle of the street and leans on the horn. On the sidewalk, two housewives with fistfuls of obnoxious bling even pause from their daily jog to watch along.

Despite the almost joyous revelry, there are constant reminders about how serious these matters are. A man named Antonio tells of his struggle with BoA, which he says tried to evict him from the home that his family's owned for 45 years. Eliza Parad, an organizer with the Chelsea Citywide Tenants Association, pulls at even heavier heartstrings. Taking the curbside podium, she speaks for a man who, after a series of health problems led to his wife's committing suicide, found a community bank that was willing to purchase his home at the market value. But BoA refused to sell, darkening an already nightmarish scenario for the family. Following a half-hour of such testimonials, the group walks off chanting a familiar cry: "WE'LL BE BACK."

READY TO RUMBLE
As you read this, hundreds of hardcore activists from across the country are arriving in Boston, where they'll be attending Right to the City's annual congress. It's no coincidence that the social and economic justice federation is convening here during the BoA protest, and the subsequent "block rebellion" on Saturday, when coalition members will hold a giant barbecue on three streets in Dorchester that have been ravaged by foreclosures and move a family into an abandoned property on NBC national news. Activists are flying in from as far as San Francisco and Miami for the purpose of helping their Boston counterparts launch the most calculated and well-publicized attack on BoA yet.

One week before the big action, MassUniting operatives hung signs outside of Kenmore Square – on both sides of the I-90 overpass – so that commuters could see their message. Last Saturday, City Life and other groups dispatched foot soldiers to go door to door around Boston, spreading the word about the upcoming rally. And back at City Life headquarters, volunteers spent Sunday afternoon in civil-disobedience training with attorneys.

MassUniting is hoping that the tactics that have been gaining ground against abusive banks here in Boston will spread to other cities.

"It's not going to be business as usual around here any more," organizer Melonie Griffiths told the standing-room crowd at City Life's September 20 bank tenant meeting.

"This foreclosure crisis has given us a new fight, and we know that we're being preyed upon," she said. "When [banks] know that a group will fight again and again, and make them look foolish, they have to deal with us. We're not the problem. The deregulation of banks is the problem."

September 27 | Day 11

A blessing this day
Cornel West speaks to GA
Takes show on the road

September 28 | Day 12

Labor days begin
Transit workers join the pack
More and more on board

September 29 | Day 13

Protests in the Bay
With Occupy Wall Street flair
Spreading like herpes

September 30 | Day 14

Occupy Boston
And like that it's a franchise
Off to the races

October 01 | Day 15

March to Brooklyn Bridge
Hundreds herded like cattle
The world is watching

October 02 | Day 16

Police learn once more
Revolution will be taped
Bridge vids go viral

October 03 | Day 17

Wall Street zombie walk
Waving 'round dead presidents
Dressed like Juggalos

October 04 | Day 18

Reno announces
Occupation coming soon
Santa Cruz starts too

October 05 | Day 19

Biggest march so far
Foley Square to Zuccotti
Cops get kettling

October 06 | Day 20

Finally some hope
Obama says he gets it
Still arrests unfold

OCCUPY BOSTON COMMON

Originally published in:
The Boston Phoenix, September 28-30, 2011

These two blog posts – blended here into a single chapter – remind me of how overwhelming it was initially to cover Occupy. On the one hand, I was trying to inform readers about a sudden phenomenon that lacked clear definition; on the other, I was struggling to understand it myself. My attitude toward Occupy was constantly shifting; I supported the overall idea, but found the meeting process so painful that I began shooting Jameson just to get through assemblies. Of course that wasn't all bad, as it gave me a chance to hang at bars with fellow hacks from other papers. In the beginning, we joked about the blind optimism on the Common, and predicted certain doom for the nascent movement; everything seemed too unfocused to sustain for long. Days turned into weeks, though, and before we caught our breath we'd stopped thinking about Occupy as one story, and started to engage it as a full-time beat.

AMERICAN BANDSTAND
September 28, 2011

At this early juncture it's fair to say that Occupy Wall Street is successful. I'm not being sarcastic. Yesterday I wrote about the media frenzy that has fertilized their protests from day one, and that's rained down even harder since police began beating demonstrators. And after last night's Occupy meeting at the Boston Common bandstand, I'm convinced that the hordes have achieved something even greater than attracting press: regardless of what they accomplish in the end, Occupy has already become the hottest protest franchise since the Tea Party. Which is why it makes sense that our rally-happy Hub is the first city to strike while the brand is hot.

Last night's kickoff testified to the weight of this movement. People have been angry for some time, but for many it was Occupy that motivated them – not the countless other protests that unfold every week around here. Roughly 300 showed – with a number of reporters also on the scene – despite the event having been announced less than a day ahead of time (Steve Annear broke the story in the *Boston Metro*). By a show of hands, a few dozen folks on the Common got their feet wet in New York at Occupy Wall Street. But for the most part, these people – mostly young, but overall from a mix of backgrounds, ages, and ethnicities – were inspired to act by what they'd seen online and in the news.

Following an introduction by organizer Robin Jacks – whose opening "Welcome to Occupy Boston" greeting may have summoned Thunderdome memories for older onlookers – an array of speakers took no longer than a few minutes apiece to chime in. Though they were asked to address Occupy priorities, many waxed extensively on tangential causes – the Fifth Amendment, capital punishment, and so on – until about a half-hour in. Then,

44

at around 8pm, the first real order of business commenced when someone asked the crowd to think about when and where they might occupy. The same speaker then detoured onto a rant about growing his own food, but he nonetheless rolled the ball in the right direction.

By a show of hands at the start of the assembly, about 20 people were interested in helping maintain a prolonged Boston occupation. But some participants got more serious as the night progressed – especially after everyone divided into working groups, and began to discuss logistical implementation issues ranging from legal, food, and medical to outreach and media. There were still some goofy moments – the night's loudest cheers came when someone screamed "Fuck capitalism!" But overall the maturity level increased over the three-plus hour congress.

Occupy Boston is already emerging as a model from which other cities might learn how to piggyback Occupy Wall Street. That's been the word on Twitter, where Hub activists have been congratulating themselves since last night, when they made the group decision to occupy Dewey Square near South Station. It's already a national movement – there are more than a dozen Occupy actions planned for now through next week, from Philadelphia to San Francisco. But from what I gather, Boston might have enough willing soldiers to become the first full-fledged expansion team.

Activists return to the Common tonight, when they'll decide when to occupy. According to Jacks (who does not speak for the entire front, but operates the @occupy_boston Twitter feed and is an "initial organizer"), some want to start this Friday (September 30), while others think they need an extra week of preparation. There's also the issue that Right to the City, MassUniting, and dozens of other groups already have massive actions planned for this weekend. But judging by the general mood, those efforts won't likely impact the decision on when to squat in Dewey Square. Most people on the Common last night didn't come to support those causes. They came to Occupy.

FIGHT THE POWER FRIDAY IS UPON US
September 30, 2011

It's not surprising that two major anti-bank actions are scheduled to rock Boston today. Still it's important to note that the demonstrations – Right to the City's massive afternoon march, and Occupy Boston's evening habitation – share no organizational ties. The former group built momentum for months, fucking with Bank of America branches from Codman Square to Cape Cod. The other front, inspired by Occupy Wall Street, popped up suddenly. But like their Right to the City counterparts, their mission is to hold greedy scumbags accountable for their crimes.

Occupy Boston's second planning powwow, held Wednesday night on Boston Common, began slowly, with about 100 people gathered near the bandstand. But the crowd soon thickened, and a show of hands revealed that there were several new recruits who'd heard about the action overnight. Of course there were also stragglers – one dude tried to sell me on the Free State Project – but the larger group was disciplined, and came to hash out issues like whether they should seek protest permits. That particular debate carried on for a tedious two hours before a majority agreed that "Egypt didn't need a permit to bring down a dictator." The next decision came quicker, as it took only minutes to reach consensus that Friday, September 30 is prime time to claim Dewey Square.

By Thursday, the soon-to-be Occupiers – all in hyper-planning mode – had lost some of their communal bliss. More than an hour of a general assembly was wasted by people flashing their intellectual cleavage before anybody addressed important items like how to handle an arrest, and how dangerous it can be to gargle pepper spray. It takes a lot of effort for this group to synthesize; a number of them have hard-willed, righteous, and even obnoxious personalities. But while many are the type of outspoken passionate souls who always irritated teachers by raising their hand too much, by the three-hour mark they were on track and tackling agenda items.

At this point reality is registering with Occupiers – particularly with city slickers who have little camping experience. Last night's torrential showers frightened some; I overheard one boyish-looking Emerson student at the final meeting – which was held indoors, at the nonprofit hub Encuentro 5 in Chinatown – tell his friends that he hadn't bothered to account for the weather. Then there's the quagmire over what kind of message the movement should adopt; last I heard, the majority wants to follow the example set by Occupy Wall Street, and identify a common cause after getting situated. Those decisions will come out of a process they call "horizontal democracy," in which everybody gets a chance to pitch change in the rhetorical jar and then vote.

Like some of the local activists who were in attendance on the Common, I was initially concerned that Occupiers might piss on Right to the City's parade. At the same time, I'm also annoyed by the fad-tastic nature of the Occupy actions, which are now spreading to several dozen cities (I'll be reporting from Occupy Miami on Saturday). Still I've decided to honor equally all of the spite aimed toward Bank of America – no matter who or where it's coming from – and at other institutions that bank big bucks on our backs. The problem up until now has been that not enough folks give a damn. That might still be the case; but in this moment, with Boston on the brink of two bloodthirsty demonstrations, it's nice to think that some State Street shitsucker on his way home to the suburbs later might be reminded of the pain he's caused.

OCCUPY THE BEACH

Originally published in:
The Boston Phoenix, October 2, 2011

No disrespect to Florida, but the place is hardly known for its progressive values. Redneck conservatives dominate the Oxycontin-soaked peninsula. Even the more mainstream Dade and Broward counties have conservative enclaves, while South Beach is to intellectuals what Boston is to supermodels. So it was to my great surprise that Occupy Miami comprised a hotbed of informed activists who were determined in spite of a political climate that burns worse than the weather. After returning from my trip to Florida, I was only in Boston for a few days before venturing back out on the road. It was hardly the Miami of Vanilla Ice, Carl Fisher, or Tony Montana, but like those ballsy bastards before me, something happened underneath the palm trees that inspired me to put it all on the line.

Most lucky reporters get to see one major movement in their lifetime. Maybe two or three in the case of a dude like R.W. Apple, or some other red-nosed journo stalwart with longevity. But in my mere half score of covering pols and pimps, contractors and detractors, whores and wars, I've already witnessed a number of full-blown culture spats, each with a cast of characters worthy of their own trading cards. From the Tea Party to al-Qaeda to the hackers who screwed Scientology, it's like I've had front row season tickets to see status quo bullshit get pounded.

All that other craziness aside, Occupy is shaping up to be the most intense beast I've ever witnessed – a multilateral thrill that's already impressed me as a person and as a writer. On one hand, I stand with any individual or entity who counters the greed and theft that's left America in shambles. On the other hand, the one with the pen in it, I'm becoming convinced that of all the mass movements I've covered, this one will grow the quickest, and become the biggest.

If I had any doubts about the Occupy promise, they were eliminated yesterday when I drove with my mom to check the first planning meeting for the budding Occupy Miami movement. I'd arranged to visit family in South Florida months ago, and considered canceling my flight to watch the Occupy Boston camp settle in on Friday. But I'm glad I didn't; what I saw on Miami Bay, in the shadow of the JFK-dedicated "Torch of Friendship," was as telling as anything I saw in Boston last week. People aren't just angry – they're angry enough to spend their weekends trying to ignite change.

With obnoxious emblems of bourgeois excess in the background – Bath & Body Works, the reprehensible Bubba Gump Shrimp Company – momentum picked up after a young guy showed up with a case of water as a support offering. That wasn't the first random act of kindness; minutes later, along with dozens of folks from every shade and age group imaginable, someone else arrived with a cooler full of soft drinks. The group of potential Occupiers here was much more diverse than Boston's bunch, consisting of fewer college students and more career activists. That's not necessarily an advantage, however, as it's clear that prolonged efforts in New York have been made possible because of youthful angst and energy.

Which raises the issue of other unique challenges that Occupy Miami will face as it enters the colossus. There are some especially depraved broods of conservatives down here that rarely breed up North – from redneck wife beaters, to pastel Palm Beach billionaires, to self-hating Latin bastards like Marco Rubio. In Miami, Tea Party puppets dominated the last mayoral elections, leaving progressives feeling, as one guy put it, "voting is meaningless in Florida." And their governor is Rick Scott, a truly special kind of scumbag.

Secondly, it's excruciatingly hot here. And when it's not hot, it's because of the sort of sporadic downpours that make Boston showers look like sponge baths. The group that showed for yesterday's powwow devoured more than three cases of water in a half-hour – making it obvious that picketers in these parts have to think about hydration first and foremost. Of course they also must consider the history between Miami cops and demonstrators – in 2003 police there brutalized hundreds who were protesting the Free Trade Area of the Americas.

Still this group has a chance. For one, they're passionate, which surprised me since I ignorantly thought that South Florida was only filled with complaining old folks and materialists. For two, Sarah Silverman can get her Jewish grandmother brigade to join the cause, like she did for Obama in '08. And third, they're following the same path to occupation that Boston activists learned from and in Liberty Square – complete with silent hand gestures, focus groups, and reliance on representative democracy. They need to tell the LaRouche piggy-backers to get lost – THEY'RE THE ASSHOLES WHO HANG POSTERS OF BARACK OBAMA WITH A HITLER MOUSTACHE – but otherwise I expect to see yesterday's group expand to occupy Miami, Fort Lauderdale, and West Palm Beach by the end of October.

Which leaves the media, and how local outlets might cover such strange events. Aside from the progressive *Miami New Times*, I'm guessing that there aren't many Huff Post columnists or *Atlantic* editors-at-large covering South Beach. Last night, the local CBS affiliate – the only television newscast to cover Occupy Miami – referred to the group as "hipsters by the Bay." I'm not one for conspiracy theories, but that label immediately preceded a commercial about how valuable Bank of America is to the local community. It was a pretty shameless, and even hilarious irony – not to mention one that will probably repeat itself from Austin to Alaska as the movement expands.

OCCUPY BOSTON GETS SERIOUS

Originally published in:
The Boston Phoenix, October 5, 2011

Like almost every blog post and feature that came after "Occupy Boston Gets Serious," I didn't really write this article alone. It's an amalgamation of my observations, input from editors, and reports from Liz Pelly and Ariel Shearer, our dedicated and embedded muckrakers who were at Dewey from the jump. Judging by the righteous gloating in this article, by this point my colleagues and I were confident in our decision to dedicate so much staff to Occupy. With news always breaking at a ludicrous speed, the whole team pooled tips and leads, and triangulated notes for accuracy. All *Phoenix* photographers and writers were encouraged to contribute. As for the quote from Mayor Tom Menino about his support for the movement . . . he gave it to me days before cops in riot gear clashed with peaceful Occupiers on his watch.

W hile they're a long way from defeating American plutocracy, Occupy Boston has accomplished a great deal in its first week. The grassroots group's downtown presence inspired not just reporters but columnists from the *Boston Globe* and *Boston Herald* to get off their ergonomic chairs and write from the field – a testament to just how far into the mainstream Occupy has buzzed since activists hit Wall Street three weeks ago. In an even greater feat, the Dewey Square squatters also spurred Fox 25 News to break from *American Idol* coverage long enough to delve into some weighty investigative reporting; on Monday, after its Beacon Hill studio was picketed by occupiers, the station filed a Freedom of Information Act request with City Hall in an effort to expose how much the occupation will cost taxpayers.

That's not all. The socially and politically diverse front of more than 100 around-the-clock occupants – plus the hundreds more who join by day or attend nighttime general assemblies (known as GAs) – established a functional frontier town on the southern tip of the Rose Kennedy Greenway. Like their Wall Street counterparts, Occupy Boston's mini-city is complete with a food pantry, infirmary, spiritual center, and media command post.

Most impressive, though, may be the group's relationship with municipal officials. In stark contrast to Manhattan, where hundreds have been arrested, here there's been real communication between agencies and occupiers, which has so far kept people safe and traffic flowing.

"We've dealt with demonstrators in the past, and we always respect their message – as long as they don't break the law," says Mayor Tom Menino. "They have to give an expression of the issues they believe in, and some of them I may happen to agree with . . . As mayor of the city, I have to respect their right to express themselves, and we'll have our police go down and work with them every day. That relationship has gone really well for us so far."

The Phoenix has been keeping tabs on Occupy since day zero – last Tuesday – when more than 200 people turned out at the Boston Common bandstand for a first planning meeting. As we reported in a series of blog posts and photo spreads, in those early stages we observed an intelligent, albeit frustrated, army of mostly college students, peppered with career activists of all ages and enough other types of characters to dispel the generic "hipster" label that some outlets have used to characterize the Wall Street Occupiers.

It's been fascinating to watch the movement mature locally. In just three days, the leaderless pack went from having no clue when or where to occupy, to negotiating with City Hall and taking Dewey Square responsibly on Friday (activists even worked with the city to arrange trash pick-up). As you read this, other sleep-ins are beginning all across the country, and the Boston group is a model assembly – the first to establish an Occupy franchise based on the Wall Street offensive. Many of their muses and organizers came directly from the New York action, where some spent more than a week in Liberty Square; but Occupy Boston has certainly taken on a unique attitude.

As has been evident at GAs – live-streamed every night on occupyboston.org – this group has its weaknesses. Whereas communication breakdowns in New York have been largely attributed to the sheer size of that occupation, Dewey Square's biggest problem appears to be finding consensus among its small but philosophically contentious gang of intellectuals and egomaniacs. Meetings often become mired in bickering over processes, while the passive-aggressive tone that dominates

GAs could rival anything you've seen on *Keeping up with the Kardashians*, or on the floor of the United States Senate for that matter.

It's hard to guess how long Occupy Boston will sustain. Its soldiers have already trudged through several days of rain and mud, not to mention a hailstorm of dismissive tweets from business brats who don't like having campgrounds visible from their financial district windows. What we do know, however, is that this movement has the potential to be the most significant populist uprising in decades, as it's already expanded to dozens of cities nationwide. Among them all, considering how things have gone so far, the Boston legion seems well-positioned for an extended haul.

Menino says Occupy Boston can stay – "as long as they don't disrupt the peace and tranquility of our city, and as long as they don't break windows and [they continue to] march with the police department overseeing them." Adds Hizzoner: "They're sending a message, like when there were demonstrations down there during Franklin Roosevelt's time. There are people getting frustrated because it seems like the government is not listening to their concerns, and this is their way of expressing themselves."

October 07 | Day 21

Mayor Bloomberg speaks
Blames Occupy for job void
And he's serious

October 08 | Day 22

Smithsonian shuts
Protest of drone strikes abroad
Occupy DC

October 09 | Day 23

Rally at White House
Conservatives infiltrate
Nobody's fooled though

October 10 | Day 24

Not such a bad day
Bloomberg says they can all stay
But arrests downtown

October 11 | Day 25

Big raid in Boston
Can't expand from Dewey Square
Vets trampled on camera

October 12 | Day 26

All eyes on the Bean
World famous lawyers take note
Hizzoner disgraced

October 13 | Day 27

Zuccotti owner
Says everyone out for scrub
People call bullshit

October 14 | Day 28

Troops parachute in
Put their bodies on the line
New York cops retreat

October 15 | Day 29

Protest in Times Square
Vet Shamar Thomas clowns cops
Instant YouTube gold

October 16 | Day 30

Chi-town under siege
Nearly two-hundred arrests
Thanks to Mayor Rahm

OCCUPATIONAL HAZARDS

Originally published in:
The Boston Phoenix, October 12, 2011

Having toured through Philly, Baltimore, and DC in their infancies, it was fascinating to watch them all grow – even from a distance – into bands of dedicated social justice advocates. Still it was odd seeing the Occupy DC warriors, on television, defending their camp in December. Since my visit two months earlier, they'd transformed from cute pimple-faced college contrarians to badass street rebels bent on holding down a giant wooden fort. Every time I saw them on a livestream – clashing at the Smithsonian, hunger-striking – I wanted to reach through the screen, pinch their cheeks, and say, "I remember when you were in diapers." As I'm putting this book to bed around the four-month anniversary of Occupy Wall Street, the DC gang is leading Occupiers from across the country to storm Congress. My, oh my, how they've grown.

*Z*uccotti Park was first. Dewey Square followed. By the time the *Phoenix* staff showed up at Occupy Boston to hold our weekly editorial meeting last Wednesday, the Boston squatters were no longer the new kids on America's occupied block – and the protest was escalating before our eyes. Occupiers were facing off with cops wielding fistfuls of plastic cuffs, busloads of union nurses were arriving, and Cornel West parachuted in to lay down some throwback Civil Rights vocals.

I looked at my editors. They looked at me. This thing was live and spreading up and down the coast like red tide. I knew there was only one thing to say: "I'll leave in the morning."

I would fly down to Washington immediately, and train and bus my way back toward the heart of the outbreak in Manhattan, stopping every place along the way where the 99 percent has taken hold. I wanted to see where it all might be headed – if, in three weeks, Occupy Boston might look like Occupy Wall Street, and if the other mass actions spawning in the Hub's wake might come to resemble the scene unfolding here.

DC: THURSDAY, OCTOBER 6
A huge anti-war, pro-jobs rally – Stop the Machine – has been planned for today since long before the Occupy movement erupted. So there are thousands of people in the streets, and somehow everybody ended up using the #OccupyDC hashtag. I walk along with them for hours, over several miles, but when the rally disperses and I finally find the real Occupy's home base in McPherson Square, it becomes clear that the residents are few and green.

The Stop the Machine folks occupying Liberty Square through Saturday shouldn't be confused with Occupy DC. Earlier in the week, Occupiers voted to remain independent, creating a small rivalry. Dozens of activists from the McPherson sect join the anti-war march, but aren't interested in an official affiliation with the group, and at one point even walk through a Stop the Machine speak-out session beating drums.

A week behind their increasingly restless Boston counterparts, the capital gang's collective attitude is still more Bob Marley than Public Enemy. The baby-faced brigade is largely comprised of politically savvy college kids from area schools. And like most of its inhabitants, Occupy DC's camp is noticeably young – it doesn't even have tents yet.

Sporting starched bandanas fresh out of the package, some undergrads use the general assembly to show off their multicultural enlightenment. A well-spoken young person in a floppy knitted hat requests that people not address others as "brothers and sisters," on account of those words not being "gender-neutral."

While this same sort of guilty-liberal grandstanding was rampant at the start of Occupy Boston, in Dewey, superfluous political correctness was sidelined days ago, as survival issues – like the question of where to house expanding forces – took precedent. But in DC, the general assembly still feels like a freshman-orientation powwow; jovial participants lounge cross-legged and listen carefully to updates without interrupting. I think about Occupy Boston's first meetings, before folks stopped being polite. Can it be that it was all so simple then?

BALTIMORE: FRIDAY, OCTOBER 7

After a short train ride from the nation's capital I arrive at McKeldin Park for Occupy Baltimore as a flamboyant blue-haired dude in an army jacket is getting walked like a poodle. He's on his hands and knees, barking at folks who are headed to and coming from the half-dozen chain eateries perched on the waterfront behind Occupy. On the other end of the leash, a brunette activist in high heels – the "cruel mistress of capitalism" – snickers at pedestrians. Unclear of what to make of the spectacle, a passerby shouts to her friends, "What the fuck are these kids doing?"

I ask the same thing, only to have a young bohemian woman in a polka-dot smock tell me it's a "Military-Industrial-Complex S&M Pageant." I should have known. It's the John Waters version of the revolution.

In addition to notable artistic flair, these Baltimoreans seem a smart group. One hula-hooping medic, a Johns Hopkins doctoral candidate named Brandie, confirms that observation by pointing to the squad's resourcefulness – they rigged a nearby fountain into sleeping quarters using boxes, foam, and blankets. There's even a hammock, which a twentysomething joker in a Cher wig says he might hijack if a rightful owner doesn't step up.

One key ingredient to Baltimore's energy is their fountain-side location, which is simultaneously located in the heart of the downtown area, and wedged between moron attractions like the Hard Rock Cafe and the financial district. They have way more foot traffic than Boston, where folks almost have to go out of their way to check the goings on up close. As a result, Baltimore has recruited a number of passers-by, while repulsing young professionals en route to Dick's Last Resort.

Like in DC, where people have yet to start acting real, the Baltimore contingent has fewer than 250 people, and is still small enough to tackle simple issues. The group's streamlined general assembly ticks like clockwork, as representatives from working groups (including food, direct action, and medical) deliver updates.

But despite the superficial manners and summer-campy feel – the latter of which is highlighted by a massive and kaleidoscopic arts-and-crafts pit in the middle of McKeldin Park – some disagreements flare up over the course of the evening. Earlier today, the group's resident anarchists painted a jumbo-sized banner that screams

"ALL COPS ARE BASTARDS." Now they want to hang it, and potentially compromise what have so far been peaceful relations with police. At one point, a granola-style activist picks a fight with a radical cop-hating long-hair. They squash the beef, agreeing to discuss the sign further at another time. Nonetheless, it's clear that the honeymoon is over.

PHILLY: SATURDAY, OCTOBER 8
Occupy Philly is like Occupy Baltimore without Ritalin, and with a whole lot more tents, people, and percussion. Just two days in, Dilworth Plaza outside of City Hall is already host to a 1000-plus Philly bash to rival Will Smith's "Summertime" video, with teach-ins in mid-lesson, animated Hare Krishnas bouncing like deflated basketballs, and an overall mood that's more festive than organized.

Even cops can't help but nod to the drum circle's rhythms, while cliques of pot crusaders, war veterans, and other breeds of radical proudly reflect on an earlier group march to the Liberty Bell. It's the party of the week; a cadre of Temple co-eds, who are not at all involved with Occupy, tell me that they came to watch the freaks before going out clubbing. They're drinking vodka cocktails out of not-so-clandestine Gatorade bottles.

This place already has the most sophisticated tech department I've seen yet – powered by eight slabs of solar thrust – and it's a good thing that they're wired. Already there is little chance of accomplishing much at Philly assemblies; tonight's devolves into poorly projected mayhem at the get-go. Around the perimeter, dozens of punks with dirty dreads and painful piercings talk over the discussion, while emotions start to fly in the front as grievances are aired over permit issues and how to picket the imperialistic Columbus Day.

I cup my ear, attempting to hear what folks are saying in the frazzled assembly, but can't make much out. So I ask a volunteer from the book table for a synopsis. He didn't hear either, but assures me that's okay. "As a group we've got no clue what the hell we're doing," he says while stroking his beard, "but there sure are a whole fucking lot of us."

WALL STREET: SUNDAY, OCTOBER 9

I'm on the Staten Island Ferry, headed to Occupy Wall Street, squeezed among a huddled mass of yuppies from the New York Road Runners Club. Their unified stench is more offensive than any homeless vegan flatulence I sniffed at various Occupy camps, as is the 'tude on two post-debutante types who are debating how to hurtle through to TriBeCa. Stepping off the boat, one says, "I'd love to cool down and walk through Battery Park, but do you think those insane people will be there yelling at everyone?"

Soon enough, aristocrats won't be able to avoid Occupy – in New York or anywhere else – as police continue cracking whips and growing small movements into major mobs. Zuccotti Park is now a settled shantytown, complete with its own classrooms, junkies, trash collectors, and daily broadsheet. The occupation continues to expand well outside of this home base, too, multiplying in spite of several hundred arrests, and spinning off offensives all across the city. Yesterday they occupied Washington Square Park due north for a rally and concert.

Bongo jam sessions still echoing between my ears, I take Monday off to spend time with family back in Queens. It's supposed to be a day of rest, writing, and grandma's meatballs, which I'm grubbing when a fellow reporter calls me from the Rose Kennedy Greenway, where this adventure began.

"Looks like you didn't need to go to Wall Street to see the action after all," he says. "A good source just told me that police are about to show up in riot gear over here – in a few hours, all eyes will be on Boston."

THE CONSENSUS KING

Originally published in:
The Boston Phoenix, October 19, 2011

C.T. Butler is a nice guy with a whole lot of patience, and a vegetarian who's not prone to fighting. Annoying. Yet I was inexorably drawn to him upon our meeting at Occupy Baltimore, so I let him talk my ear off for more than an hour. As it turns out, Butler helped found the influential anarchist force Food Not Bombs in Cambridge years ago, but was living in obscurity until Occupy moved him to resurface. "The Consensus King" is a comeback story; while I saw a lot of older activists fail to reach young Occupiers, Butler wound up getting invites to camps across the country. He hit some snags; on one occasion, a disgruntled Boston Occupier even threatened Butler for telling him to wait his turn. But unlike a lot of his contemporaries, he ultimately earned respect in the movement by practicing the consensus gospel that he preaches.

C.T. Lawrence Butler hasn't been to Boston in nearly a decade. Yet it takes the godfather activist fewer than five seconds to get his bearings when he steps off the train from Baltimore.

Emerging from South Station, Butler strides toward Occupy Boston's tent city, wheeling a suitcase filled with books, handouts, and other weapons against mass oppression. A progressive icon who co-founded Food Not Bombs (FNB) in the 1980s, Butler has entangled his five-foot-seven frame in enough police beatings to cause post-traumatic stress disorder. He knows his way around a protest.

Butler came to lend the occupiers support. But now he stops in his tracks. He recognizes the landscape and suddenly realizes he fought on the same battlefield three decades ago.

"This is where it all began," he says, pointing to the Federal Reserve Bank of Boston. "Right over there, on the lawn outside of that big oppressive building, was where we had our first Food Not Bombs feed in March of 1981."

But the association goes far deeper than that coincidence of history. In many ways, the Occupy movement is the flowering of seeds that Butler planted decades ago. He wrote the book on consensus-making – literally. Ideas from his flagship work, *On Conflict and Consensus*, are staples of the democratic decision-making process as it's practiced in Occupy camps from the Bay Area to Baltimore. Similarly, the 1992 Food Not Bombs handbook, which Butler co-authored with fellow FNB co-founder Keith McHenry, provides a sort of blueprint for large-scale actions like Occupy, in which facilitators are challenged to synthesize wildly diverse groups of varying interests.

As he walks into the camp, no one recognizes him. He's just another protestor. But he can't help but marvel at the manifestation of his life's work.

"I'd like to think that I have something to do with this," he says.

CHARMED LIFE

Butler enjoyed a charmed artistic life until the 1980s. The Delaware-cum-Long Island native lived on Beacon Hill, and helped manage the Charles Playhouse in the nearby theater district. He also produced plays, mostly of the pop-intellectual type, which he put on at Boston Center for the Arts, among other venues. But that all changed on May 24, 1980, when he joined thousands of other young people in storming the construction site of the future Seabrook nuclear station.

Three years earlier, in 1977, more than 1400 anti-nuke activists, aligned with the legendary Clamshell Alliance, were arrested for setting up a tent city at Seabrook. The 1980 action that Butler participated in was a last-ditch effort to rekindle the Clamshell legacy by occupying the facility. But New Hampshire state police, along with the National Guard, had a different plan: as soon as protesters sliced through fences and entered the property, troops pounced on the crowd, spraying tear gas and beating people senseless. Butler avoided physical injury, but says the assaults nonetheless left lasting marks.

"I didn't even go to Seabrook for the politics," says Butler. His father was a white-collar administrator for the military defense contractor Thiokol, and Butler recalls his family as being non-political. "I went down there for the drama, and out of curiosity, and to be a part of it all. I had no idea that my life would never be the same after that – that's when I became an activist."

In a story that you might hear old radicals recite over lagers at the Plough and Stars in Cambridge, Butler – along with six other FNB founders, including McHenry – spun the energy they harnessed at Seabrook into a food collection and distribution charity. They orchestrated a successful defense for Brian Feigenbaum – their friend, legal advisor, and future FNB collaborator who was arrested at Seabrook for allegedly hurling a grappling hook at a police officer. After that win, the team began preparing regular meals for the homeless, and feeding protesters at demonstrations from New Hampshire to New York City. They also grew close personally, living together in a life cooperative at 195 Harvard Street, near Central Square.

Butler, also a member of the City of Cambridge Peace Commission at the time, worked with FNB until 1983. That year, he went on to co-found Food for Free, an FNB offshoot that still provides needy people around Greater Boston with more than one million pounds of meals a year. After leaving the Boston area in 1987, Butler continued protesting power and corruption, and often squatted in San Francisco, where he and a relocated McHenry revitalized FNB to grow it westward. After violent arrests in response to their peaceful actions spurred a wave of sympathetic news coverage, the pair succeeded in expanding Food Not Bombs to more than 30 American cities.

In the time since, Butler has stayed off the front lines and mostly focused on teaching consensus-making. For the past three years, he's lived with his partner, the magnificently dreadlocked Wren Tuatha, in a Maryland community called Heathcote, where the couple teaches peaceful communication. Butler never expected to step back into the protest arena; his post-traumatic stress disorder – the result, he says, of being placed in Vulcan-grip compliance holds and knocked unconscious several times – has kept him away from big crowds and mass actions for years. That all changed when he heard about Occupy.

PICKET-LINE REUNION

I first met Butler at Occupy Baltimore, where I'd stopped on my tour of five Occupy camps in search of the big picture. He was an outsider, having just shown up in McKeldin Square for the first time that afternoon. But by the time that I returned for the nightly general assembly, Butler had been invited to address the entire group. Having been told that earlier Baltimore meetings were compromised by out-of-turn dissent and soapbox soliloquies, he used the platform to teach young activists how to find consensus in affinity groups before uniting for assemblies. "If an idea doesn't work in a group of 10 people," he told the attentive crowd, "it definitely won't work in a group of 200."

Now Butler hopes to bring that message to Boston, and to any other Occupy cities that will hear him out. This past weekend, he and Tuatha introduced themselves to everyone around Dewey Square who would listen. Butler was given a table inside camp to distribute tracts on consensus techniques, and spent most of Saturday schooling young people and greeting old friends who'd come out for an anti-war rally that afternoon. Back in the area for the first time in years, he now hopes to get the band back together. Anne Shumway, an old-time picket-line co-defendant, becomes animated at the sight of Butler: "We got arrested together for years," she tells everyone in earshot. "And look at us now – we're still doing this."

After that reunion and others, Butler crosses to the other side of Atlantic Avenue. There, on the bench area outside the Federal Reserve Bank, Occupy Boston has scheduled him to lead a workshop in consensus decision-making. A dozen people show up. He'd hoped for a bigger turnout, but didn't expect to suddenly become the focal point of a movement that's grown into the thousands. Still, he shares stories of effective practices, and asks the small group to spread the word that he'll be back in two weeks.

Toward the end of his talk, a fleet of motorcycle cops that was idling in front of the reserve building takes off to follow college students on a march. Butler eyes the entrance to the Federal Reserve, the place where it all began.

"Now's our chance," he jokes. "I've been waiting 30 years for this – let's storm this place."

INSIDE THE OCCUPY MEDIA STRUGGLE

Originally published in:
The Boston Phoenix, October 26, 2011

For a self-styled "leaderless" movement, it's been obvious since day one that some Occupiers work harder than others, and that those decision-makers run point on a number of fronts. When Occupy Boston started – and this goes for every city that I visited – those de-facto generals steered the media team. Those who disseminated info from the camps handled duties that would have challenged seasoned PR maestros, at one point processing hundreds of press inquiries a day, and helping link journalists with Occupiers. As a reporter, I'm not supposed to get along with flacks. But while I take pride in my somewhat contentious relationship with Occupy's media reps, I'll raise a glass any day to the movement's reliable spokespeople, who, at least on a whole, I found to be more transparent than most spinmeisters I've encountered through the years.

It's a familiar scene outside the Occupy Boston media tent: a local television news reporter and her cameraman approach cautiously, looking for a clue. They inch up to the closed zipper door, and the talent cups her ear to check if anyone's inside. She hears voices, and softly says, "Um . . . hello? Anybody who can help with media requests in there?"

The zipper opens halfway, and a twentysomething with an Einstein 'fro pokes his melon out like the Wonderful Wizard. He removes his shades, inspects the newswoman in her skirt suit, and says nothing. The reporter asks, "Is there someone who does interviews?" To which the Occupier responds, before disappearing back into his weatherproof bunker, "Anyone can talk to you – but they only speak for themselves."

Unlike welcome desks at political conventions, at Occupy Boston there are no credentials, gift bags, or lanyards stitched with corporate logos. The sign out front this tent might say MEDIA, but in reality it hosts a hodgepodge battalion of social-networking flacks, programmers and spin surgeons, in-house hacks and bloggers – a squad that isn't in business to service the mainstream media.

Participants like Nadeem Mazen – an MIT grad and owner of a Cambridge tech consulting firm who's been a de facto mouthpiece for the movement from early on – have indeed granted hundreds of outside interviews. But in those exchanges and through their own outlets, vols primarily focus on disseminating news from the general Occupy perspective, and on correcting what they consider to be misinformation.

Though still in dire need of outside contributions, Occupy Boston media has come a long way since last month, when their whole output consisted of a Twitter feed and a Facebook page. Still, the ensemble force is not yet the dynamic machine needed for this sort of massive operation – especially if there's no coherent, unified message to push. Also discouraging is that Occupy Boston media has suffered from an identity crisis, as the team was initially formed to handle an impossible range of tasks, from technological needs to public relations.

At this time, the group lacks adequate tools, manpower, and capability, as the majority of occupiers don't have laptops or smart phones. According to Mazen, the team is still far from being able to process revolution in real time. Robin Jacks, a 31-year-old Occupy activist who earned her stripes backing lefty causes in her native Memphis, agrees that there are limitations, but says it's important to note the velocity at which they hit the ground running. "Every day people ask us, 'What's your message?'" says Jacks. "We're working on that, but it takes time. Other movements had months or even years to figure these things out. We're just getting started."

UNDER SIEGE
The media team's first big test came in the late hours of Columbus Day, when police descended on the Rose Kennedy Greenway to arrest Occupy squatters who'd staged a secondary camp. Under siege, the team furiously gathered footage and information, and by any measure handled the crisis competently, shaping the emerging narrative according to their experience.

As cops approached the perimeter, Jacks bolted to a nearby safe-house and began tweeting. Mazen stayed on the front lines shooting video, while operatives by his side relayed messages to those in remote locations. Gregg Housh, a Web wiz famous for his role in the hacker group Anonymous's war on Scientology, rented a 12th-floor room at the Intercontinental Hotel to record an aerial view.

In the middle of it all, the group got a resounding boost from liberal icon and Current TV personality Keith Olbermann, who tweeted, "For those asking 'where is the media coverage of the police riot at #OccupyBoston' – Twitter IS the media coverage. Follow @Occupy_Boston." Within hours, the @Occupy_Boston following tripled from 5000 to 15,000.

Without much infrastructure in place – its primary Web site, occupyboston.org, was still in early stages of development – the media team found itself the focus of national attention. Swooping in to help, veteran Web activists from groups like the Independent Media Center and Global Revolution, both of which had already helped power Occupy Wall Street's message, also put Boston on full blast.

When the smoke cleared, the media troop had dominated the online conversation – or, as Housh puts it, instead of telling "corporate media to go fuck itself," they "got them to report what Occupy Boston wanted them to report." Adds Jacks: "We didn't even have to spin things, because we're the ones being spun on."

LEARNING CURVE
Despite the viral myth that there was a media "blackout" at the beginning of Occupy Wall Street, there were in fact hundreds of stories posted during the first days that protesters took Zuccotti Park – including sympathetic coverage from such mainstream outlets as the *Guardian* and ABC. So by the time that Occupy hit Boston two weeks later, local, national, and even international media were poised to swarm like paparazzi.

Occupy Wall Street's media ops have come under scrutiny, with a widely syndicated Associated Press story from last week noting a "chaotic and complicated relationship with [outside] media." In their turn, Occupy Boston has tried to learn from New York's PR wins and errors. Gunner Scott, a seasoned activist and executive director of the Massachusetts Transgender Political Coalition, has handled the bulk of the press releases. Recently, multiple Twitter jockeys were finally given access to all house accounts, so that they can crowd-source coverage and amplify concurrent happenings.

In the coming weeks, the media team plans to conduct internal demographic surveys in order to help outside outlets get their facts straight. Mazen also says they'll concentrate on disseminating more videos. All this while press inquiries haven't slowed down – they still get dozens of calls every day, and spend time correcting lazy journalists and deflecting slanderous conservative trolls.

One month in, Occupy Boston media still has yet to hone its purpose – not unexpected considering the New York theater's continuing ambiguity. But they are aware of their shortcomings, the most significant of which is a glaring digital divide among Occupiers. Despite the Limbaugh line that they all pack iPhones, most Dewey Square campers lack Web access. Technological inequities have even caused breakdowns; just last week the media tent was occupied by members of the direct-action committee, who demanded more access to electricity.

One protester looking to address digital disparities is Dan Schneider, an Emerson senior who launched the *Boston Occupier.* Similar to Zuccotti's *Occupied Wall Street Journal,* he says the newspaper will present a balanced voice that reflects experiences of activists in Dewey Square and elsewhere. Next week Schneider will use more than $8000 that he raised on Kickstarter to distribute copies of his paper around camp and throughout the city – a move that might seem backward for a group that's often hailed as "Web-savvy" and "nu-media literate." But according to those who have weathered the storm so far, their success moving forward depends on the extent to which the whole movement stays informed.

"For a long time, we were saying that there weren't enough people of color, or enough LGBTQ people," says Mazen. "But overall we're also working with people who barely text, let alone vote on a Wiki. If we really want to represent the 99 percent, we have to think about how we can disseminate through low-tech means. It's like a lot of other things: we're working on it, but we just haven't gotten there yet."

October 17 | Day 31

Reporter is fired
Precedent is now set for
Occu-journalists

October 18 | Day 32

Jon Stewart is back
The Daily Show now believes
Offers some advice

October 19 | Day 33

Occupy Des Moines
Crashes DNC HQ
Equal opp gadflies

October 20 | Day 34

NPR journo
Axed from the program Soundprint
The trend continues

October 21 | Day 35

Occupy The Hood
Boston speak-out in Dudley
Huge Dewey turnout

October 22 | Day 36

Screw you Wells Fargo
Occupy Philly bank jam
Mission accomplished

October 23 | Day 37

Sacramento fun
In name of First Amendment
Twenty-three get cuffed

October 24 | Day 38

Chicago action
Hundred-plus jailed while shouting
Hell no we'll be back

October 25 | Day 39

Scott Olsen attacked
Another Iraq War vet
Returns to combat

October 26 | Day 40

Rallies for Olsen
Rage all across the country
Vet in critical

November 6, 2011

Occupy News

Occupy Boston Resolves Legal Dispute

Last night the General Assembly welcomed Paul Carnes and Sydney Sherrell back to Occupy Boston with open consensus hands followed by an announcement by the Financial Accountability Working Group (FAWG) of Occupy Boston. The announcement stated that Carnes and Sherrell have reached an agreement with members of the financial working group on behalf of Occupy Boston to work out their differences after weeks of a communication break-down and an intensive mediation lead by the attorney David Kelston. Over 150 news articles and blog post were written about this issue alone.

Occupy Boston started out strong, hopeful, and ambitious. This is a new and young movement that will have bumps in the road. We're becoming stronger everyday. When Carnes and Sherrell took to the stage at the General Assembly, it was clear that lessons have been learned, their motives were pure at heart, and they truly care about the occupation.

The entirety of the Occupation Movement is filled with people who are dedicated to see this revolution succeed. These are people who put their lives on hold, quit their jobs to devote all their time to the Movement, and vacated their homes to live in a tent. The goal is to unite together and fight for what we believe, in solidarity for the good of us all. Both Carnes and Sherrell came to an agreement with Occupy Boston to do just that. All is live and well in Occupy Land.

WHO IS PAUL FETCH?

Originally published in:
The Boston Phoenix, November 14, 2011

This whole book could have been about Paul Fetch. Or Paul Carnes. Or whatever the fuck his name is. Of all the intriguing characters I've met over the last few months, the accused Occupy Boston embezzler may be the most worthy of a bio-pic. I heard stories elsewhere about small-time crooks who took advantage of the movement's vulnerable operations. But while those sketchballs allegedly stole more than anyone accused Carnes of taking, they don't compare to Dewey's hallmark huckster. At one point, Carnes even sued Boston Occupiers for banning him – an honor to which he and his homegirl, Sydney Sherell, can lay exclusive claim. He also has another accolade in his honor; of all the ink I spilled about Occupy, Fetch is the only individual whose antics warranted a feature-length treatment.

In his first few weeks at Occupy Boston, Paul Carnes was just another face in the horde, an affable 27-year-old with a sweet Southern accent. He dressed differently than most Dewey Square squatters – favoring dress shirts and neckties – but otherwise fit right in, assisting with everything from logistics to heavy lifting. Media outlets sometimes requested interviews with Carnes due to his preppy flare, but he largely avoided the spotlight, preferring to help campers set up tents. Along with his close friend Sydney Sherell, he also liked to spend hours at the information desk – a default greeting post for visitors and donors.

Though they have come to perceive him as a grifter and the oddest Occupy adversary imaginable, most who can recall his early movements claim Carnes first came off as an average protester, going through the daily picket motions and crashing in a small tent with Sherell at night. If anything seemed strange at all, it was his vocal dislike of the movement's every-voice-counts mantra. Occupy runs on an equal-opportunity structure called "horizontal democracy." Carnes focused on smaller working groups and sat out the more formal general assemblies (GAs).

When the GA voted to streamline fundraising efforts three weeks into the occupation, Carnes jumped at the chance to take financial control where he saw possible. Up until that point, each working group had its own donation box, so people could give to the medical team at the first-aid tent, to the tech squad at the media tent, and so forth. In its attempt at transparency, the assembly finally established a central collection hub and Financial Accountability Working Group (FAWG) to oversee fiscal operations. Carnes volunteered to help the effort, agreeing to guard cash donations and sign his name on bank accounts. He assured people that he could handle such duties on account of his studying at Harvard Business School – even though he never matriculated there.

But less than a week after Carnes took over camp finances, FAWG issued a press release stating that Carnes and Sherell had been expelled from the group due to "lack of accountability and transparency, as well as their failure to provide information to both the FAWG and the General Assembly." Accusers charged Carnes with refusing to share paperwork for a City of Boston "Doing Business As" (DBA) certificate that he established (with the group's permission) for Occupy Boston, and for an account that he opened at Liberty Bay Credit Union. Gripes were also made about receipts found in the cash box for which Carnes was responsible; hundreds of dollars' worth of purchased items were unaccounted for, and he appeared to be treating himself to meals and snacks near Dewey Square. Lastly, members of FAWG realized that the smooth talker from Alabama who called himself Paul Carnes also had a second identity – the guy with the keys to their account was also a notorious online anti-hero named Paul Fetch.

Nearly two weeks after the Carnes controversy compromised Occupy Boston's morale and reputation – the movement's financial irresponsibility and lackadaisical vetting of Carnes were noted by a number of news sources, including this one – it appears that accountability has been somewhat restored. Following several meetings with a legal mediator, Carnes and Sherell handed the DBA and bank account over to FAWG, and were in turn permitted to remain at Occupy Boston (until the GA banned them outright last Thursday). It was a cheap lesson; though Carnes denies embezzling funds, many with direct knowledge of the situation say that he misappropriated no more than $500, and perhaps also allegedly pocketed about that much from cash donations.

It's inherently fascinating that a movement spawned from outrage over greed was tainted by thievery. That's certainly the irony that most media has focused on in reporting fiscal improprieties at Occupy Wall Street and elsewhere. What's as noteworthy, though, are the infrastructural inadequacies that make so many occupations vulnerable. In Dewey Square, Carnes was able to charm his way into a de facto CFO role – that despite his bizarre history as an unhinged viral Web antagonist who once clashed with, then claimed to be the leader of, the faceless hacktivist collective Anonymous (he's not – they have no leader, nor did they ever). Had Occupiers done their homework – i.e., googled him – they'd have thought sooner to keep extra eyeballs on the sharp dresser with the charming drawl.

PLAYING FETCH

Since his childhood, Carnes has been crusading for one cause or another. He grew up in Dothan, Alabama – a city of 65,000, wedged between Georgia and the Florida panhandle, that calls itself the "Peanut Capital of the World." There, a young Carnes was active with the Ridgecrest Southern Baptist Church, and as a teenager participated in a program that brought him up and down the East Coast pitching gospel door to door. On one of those trips, he told a reporter with a Baptist newspaper that traveling allowed him to meet the kinds of people who he couldn't find in Dothan.

Years later, after studying business and theater at Chipola College in northern Florida, Carnes returned home with a left-leaning agenda, joining the Alabama Democratic State Executive Committee in 2006. He also grew active in his local LGBT community, and that year was named the southeast coordinator for the equal-rights group Equality Alabama. A skilled fundraiser, Carnes helped Birmingham state representative Patricia Todd become the first ever openly gay pol to win office in Alabama.* An employee of that state's Democratic party, who declined to speak on the record, says he remembers Carnes as a hard worker and ambitious campaigner.

Despite a promising career in local party politics, Carnes was determined to make his mark beyond the Peanut Capital. In a low-budget Web reality show that he developed three years ago called *Your Reality*, Carnes says, straight-faced, that "Alabama is ready to compete with Hollywood, we're ready to compete with New York, we're ready to compete with London, we're ready to compete with anybody out there." Wearing a blue blazer and gray Dockers, sipping a blood-red cocktail out of a trashy-chic martini glass with a busty blonde beside him, Carnes invites the world to watch, boasting lower Alabama as the premier place where hot young people "need to be."

Around the same time, Carnes established his alter ego, and began posting YouTube rants under the handle Mr. Fetch. Unlike his attempt at reality-show stardom, the clips of Carnes melodramatically reeling in his bedroom, bath, and kitchen did earn him a relatively significant degree of fame. In 2008 he uploaded a video titled "ANONYMOUS Stand Down!!!", in which he blasted the ubiquitous hacker group best known for waging street and cyber war on the Church of Scientology. The clip features Carnes, sporting a white wife-beater and with images of murderous jihadists edited in behind him, hollering that Anonymous is "evil," and accusing them of burning houses down. "Let me tell you something," warns Carnes. "This is your one chance to surrender . . . If you don't stand down, we will be left with no other choice but to unite as one tube together and fight you!"

It's unclear whether Carnes knew who he was fucking with; judging by the multiple amateurish Web sites he manages for various causes, his computer skills would hardly put him in the general Anon echelon. Nonetheless, his anti-Anonymous debut – and follow-ups like "ANONYMOUS Where's Yo Brain At?" – were enough to poke the hornet's nest, and the Internets fired back with a vengeance. Within days, dozens of spoof and threat videos took aim at Carnes, and offended Anons broadcasted his family's personal info on chat boards, right down to Social Security numbers and insurance-access codes. The group became so pre-occupied with Carnes – calling his house, soiling his online identity – that one video, made by an Anon for other Anons, begged legionnaires to "not fall for his meager tricks . . . for [they are] having a devastating impact on this organization and its people."

Instead of taking a hint, Carnes saw opportunity in the proudly leaderless Anonymous, and attached himself to it like a boil. Carnes began declaring himself as the head of Anonymous. As recently as a few months ago, he claimed to have helped Anonymous hack entities ranging from the FBI and CIA to Bank of America. In a September presentation at the Boston New Tech Meetup, held at Microsoft in Cambridge, Carnes claimed that Anonymous had "grown up" since he took the helm. "They might embarrass you," he said, "but they're not going to blow up your house or anything."

Organizers of the Boston New Tech Meetup say that the crowd couldn't figure what to think of the self-proclaimed hack star and his lack of basic Web knowledge. But that's a common reaction to Carnes, whose online persona morphs regularly from religious zealot to motivational speaker to crazed slayer-turned-leader of Anonymous. Even Gawker took notice of the bipolar fantasies that he embraces with the gusto of a kid playing cops and robbers, and in 2008 ran a blog post titled, "Paul Fetch Is the New Andy Kaufman. Unless He's Just Really Really Unfunny." The article pondered: "If the videos by this YouTube user are parodies, and his entire online persona is a character, then we must all bow down to the new king . . . But chances are he's just a terribly unfunny douche."

'THEY FORCED OUR HAND'

The motions to excommunicate Sherell and Carnes from the Occupy Boston financial working group began just days after they'd signed on. Other members of FAWG were having trouble contacting them, and the pair ditched a meeting in which they were supposed to hand over the DBA and credit-union account info with which they could access donations. After several failed attempts to reach Carnes, FAWG operatives finally called Sherell, who they say answered but was taking cues from someone in the background. Instead of meeting with the group, Sherell said she and Carnes were going shopping for tents – even though no such spree had been approved by the assembly.

Receipts show that Carnes did in fact spend more than $400 in cash at an army supply store on Mass Ave that evening. There he purchased boots, flags, coats, and other items, only some of which were ever accounted for by FAWG, which, upon realizing Carnes's unreliability, removed about $2000 in cash donations from Carnes and Sherell's tent. Their concerns were piqued when they discovered that Carnes had been attempting to gain control over a number of working groups, and falsely told organizers that he had permission to obtain passwords to their Web sites, e-mail accounts, and social networks.

Especially troubling was word that Carnes had attempted to run a similar scam in Cleveland two weeks earlier. According to Rebecka Hawkins, a legal observer with the Ohio outfit, Carnes showed up on the third day of Occupy Cleveland claiming to have been dispatched from Boston and the National Lawyers Guild to help campers get organized (neither is true). Hawkins says Carnes tried rallying troops into imprudent and premature acts of civil disobedience, and furthermore refused to bring decisions to the whole group – all of which prompted an investigation. "He kept saying, 'Boston's going to look unfavorably at you,' and that made us really suspicious," says Hawkins. "We thought he was a plant for some government organization. But when we looked him up online, it turns out he has a history of being a nut job."

FAWG announced on October 24 that Carnes and Sherell were banned from handling camp monies. "They forced our hand," group member Greg Murphy told the GA. "It was unanimous – they've lost the trust of all of us." Coming to his own defense, Carnes announced that he'd planned – on his own initiative – an Occupy anniversary party for that weekend at the Boston Teacher's Union hall in Dorchester. (He had, in fact, rented a room at the BTU, but received permission from neither the union nor Occupy Boston to organize a joint celebration. BTU President Richard Stutman says Carnes did try to make inroads, though, claiming to have once worked for the Alabama Department of Education.) Outraged, some Occupiers screamed at the accused embezzler, especially when he confessed to having not attended a single GA since arriving more than three weeks earlier. To make matters worse, after two minutes Carnes stormed off to the information tent, where he demanded dinner (which he was given) and requested individual meetings with each of his accusers.

The day after Carnes and Sherell were exposed, a team of eight FAWG members – some college students, a few older professionals, two attorneys – met at an off-site location to fix the mess left in the wake of the pair's antics, and to protect the more than $25,000 that Occupy Boston had so far raised. For starters, they agreed to conduct background checks on all FAWG members, and to buy a more secure cash box. But there was one looming problem – Carnes was still in possession of Occupy Boston's DBA certificate and credit-union documents. After considering a lawsuit, they decided to ask if Carnes would resolve things through a mediator.

Carnes agreed to mediation, and the first session lasted more than four hours. He and Sherell insisted on retaining permission to fundraise for Occupy Boston, and, to the horror of FAWG members,

Carnes proposed that he get to keep 20 percent of donations he could solicit (by this time he'd redesigned his personal Web page, paulcarnes.com, to raise funds for Occupy efforts in more than a dozen cities). Carnes also insisted that FAWG publicly exonerate him and Sherell at the next GA. Their hands tied, after two days FAWG met them halfway, agreeing to release a statement that the matter was resolved in exchange for the DBA and account numbers. Sherell and Carnes would be allowed to stay at camp, and even to attend FAWG meetings without voting power.

News that Carnes hadn't been expelled disturbed a number of Occupiers, some of whom promptly drafted a proposal to ban him from Occupy Boston forever. His appearance and attempt at reconciliation at a subsequent GA was equally scorned, and by that time his tent had been broken down and stashed away by angry campers. Still, Carnes stuck around, and the day after was hanging with Sherell and two other Occupiers across the street from camp, handing out pieces of paper that read, "Occupy News … Last night the General Assembly welcomed Paul Carnes and Sydney Sherell back to Occupy Boston with open consensus-hands." Asked which Occupy media group produced the article, he said he couldn't remember. Nevertheless, Carnes insisted that the leaflet cleared his name.

"If someone wants to throw something at me, I can deal with it," said Carnes. "But I believe in this movement. I believe that it's bigger than this situation and bigger than Occupy Boston – there are occupations all over the world now. I want to be involved as much as possible, and I see myself working on more of a global level. This is just a bump in the road. In a few days, I'm going to Wall Street."

By the time that the GA banned him from Occupy Boston the next night, he'd already left to occupy Manhattan.

* *I did a good amount of diligence in researching Carnes – calling old associates in his native Alabama, digging up newspaper clippings about his involvement in church and LGBT groups. But investigating a character like him is tough, since he's apparently fooled countless people – including me. Though Carnes claims to have helped the first openly gay politician in his home state get elected – and was listed as having done so in his bio for Boston Pride's Latino Pride Committee which he served on – it turns out to be another stretch. "I can assure you that he did NOT raise a dime, nor did he work in my campaign," Representative Patricia Todd wrote me in an email after reading my article. "I know Paul from his work in LGBT issues, although to say "work" is really not true. He has a loud voice and is a lone wolf and not a team player!"*

OCCUPY THE HOOD BOSTON

ROXBURY | DORCHESTER | MATTAPAN | SOUTH END | JP | HYDE PARK | ROSLINDALE

BLACK-UPY BOSTON: BLACK | LATINO | CAPE VERDEAN

DEWEY SQUARE TO DUDLEY SQUARE

FRI. OCT. 21, 2011 | 6 PM

OCCUPY THE HOOD I BOSTON

Originally published in:
The Boston Phoenix, October 18, 2011

I'm not wholly surprised that things didn't jibe between Occupy Boston and Jamarhl Crawford, the Roxbury activist behind Beantown's Occupy the Hood actions. Some management styles are just incompatible, and Crawford's not the only community advocate who was turned off by Occupy's horizontal democracy model, if not by the endless general assemblies and their passive-aggressive undertones. But despite communication difficulties, the introduction of Dewey dwellers to Roxbury in October helped spawn important relationships down the line. In one respect, this interview highlights issues which still need to be addressed by Occupy. At the same time, it shows how Occupiers and outside organizers – in Boston and elsewhere – might be able to move past academic grandstanding and initiate a more honest discussion about race.

Last Tuesday, Roxbury rabble-rouser Jamarhl Crawford finally addressed the Occupy Boston general assembly. Indeed, it seemed only a matter of time before the *Blackstonian* editor and activist became attracted to the momentum on Dewey Square; the crowd downtown is screaming for many – if not all – of the same issues that he's been mobilizing on for years.

Like many of the Occupy legionnaires, Crawford is skeptical of authority figures. More specifically, he's one of the few outspoken critics of Boston Police Department behavior, recently coordinating actions in response to Suffolk County District Attorney Dan Conley's controversial findings on the 2010 arrest and brutal beat-down of a 16-year-old male at Roxbury Community College.

Furthermore, Crawford tends to draw ire from the same conservative hemorrhoids that are up in Occupy's ass. Which is why there's already been a flurry of online swipes – some tongue-in-cheek, others downright racist – since he announced official plans to occupy Dudley Square on Friday night.

Similarities aside, Occupy Boston and Occupy the Hood need more than just common enemies if they plan to coalesce. There's been a lot of talk about diversifying camps here and elsewhere, but what will it take for that to really happen? We asked Crawford what the "'hood" can bring to the budding Occupy movement, in Boston and beyond, and what communities of color should expect in return.

When were you approached to go down to Occupy Boston?

I wasn't approached. Initially I had no plans of going down there because nothing was speaking to me, but I finally did after much trepidation, and after people I know and trust went down and reported positive things back to me.

What were your observations on racial and ethnic diversity down there?

Diversity was almost non-existent. On top of that everyone was being too polite – no one was saying what they really think. The polite conversations have gotten us nowhere – they've gotten us to assimilation, co-optation, and infiltration. If white people are truly sincere about wanting us to be a part of this, then they have to be willing to endorse whatever it is that we do – without judgment, and without suggestions about how the actions should take shape. They can either come as observers, or as supporters – that's fine either way. They don't have to come silently, though, because when we say, 'Can you feel that?' – we want them to say, 'Fuck yeah!'

What opportunities did you see at Occupy Boston?

I saw the clusterfuck, but I also saw that this moment was pregnant with potential. A lot of people didn't know what was going on as far as issues that I'm concerned about, but when I expressed what I thought would be some good moves, they listened, and they seemed to like the idea that they should do something in communities of color. Like I said, they need to be in support of current organizational efforts that are already pre-existing, because people have been doing this work for years, on everything from police brutality to educational disparities.

There seemed to be a big response to your call to occupy foreclosed homes in the black community. What exactly do you mean by that?

There's a list of foreclosed homes, and a lot of those homes are concentrated in the black community, where there's been a huge impact – whole streets are condemned. If [Occupy Boston] wants to do something in communities of color – I said that they should occupy some of these spots. Because if anybody's getting fucked, we're getting fucked the worst. Our mortgage loans are higher, and we get foreclosed on at a higher rate. On top of that, we have to deal with having all these abandoned homes in our communities. Some of the foreclosed houses were the nicest homes on their street, and now they're overgrown and disregarded. I wish the banks maintained their properties, since they have more money than the people who used to live there. But they don't, and now foreclosures are the new crackhouses – the most fucked up homes on the street. These banks take no ownership, they don't cut the grass, and as a result the whole neighborhood is more susceptible to break-ins, fires, and you name it. It's a problem.

What should Occupy Boston activists consider if they want to attract communities of color?

They should think about what it's like for a dude like me – from the 'hood, with the experience that I have – listening to a 24-year-old white kid talking about being brutalized by the police when they started arresting people [on the Rose Kennedy Greenway]. Did any of them get killed? No. But where I'm from people really do get brutalized and killed by police. I hear what they're talking about, but it's a different level of shit. They need to realize that no matter what issue they're worried about, my people probably suffer from it at an exponentially higher rate than the rest of the population.

What can the black community bring to Occupy Boston?

On the community end, a lot of people who are on board have already been working on these issues. They've been organizing in the 'hood. Together, we're going to continue to organize, and hopefully this is the time for us to find common ground and use our momentum to show people that the entire world is tired of the shit that's been going down.

What exactly is Occupy the Hood, as far as the specific actions are concerned?

Friday night you'll see a community speak-out with multiple organizations and individuals who will speak to their own issues – the issues they know best. I'll also have politicians there – that's something I haven't seen much of [at Occupy Boston]. As long as you have a legitimate issue, a track record, and have been working on that issue, then rock on – please. People have been asking, 'What's it going to be?' And we've been asking them, 'What are you going to do when you get there?'

Will this just be a one night thing?

No. We've already been doing this work, and we'll continue doing more of it in the future. Moving forward with Occupy the Hood, though, I promise that a lot of people will be surprised by the places we decide to show up and occupy.

October 27 | Day 41

Oakland mayor caves
Pressure crashing down the coast
Occupiers mount

October 28 | Day 42

Crackdown in Tuscon
Tally close to four-hundred
They're everywhere now

October 29 | Day 43

One more brutal day
Occupy Denver blasted
Pepper bullets fly

October 30 | Day 44

Austin protesters
Trying to feed hungry folks
Result thirty jailed

October 31 | Day 45

Trick or Occupy
Guy Fawkes masks everywhere
Scream guy hangs it up

November 01 | Day 46

CEO to speak
At Wash U in Seattle
Mic check motherfuck

November 02 | Day 47

General strike time
Oakland breaks new boundaries
Tear gas and ports shut

November 03 | Day 48

Oakland is on fire
Flash bang grenades riot cops
Bad for tourism

November 04 | Day 49

Occupy Tulsa
Bastion of intolerance
Twenty-three arrests

November 05 | Day 50

Remember the fifth
Guy Fawkes Day celebration
Mad pranks plus change banks

OCCUPY THE UPPER EAST SIDE

Unpublished:
November 13, 2011

This piece about Occupy Wall Street never ran in the *Phoenix* for two reasons. First, I filed the draft right before the big police raid on Zuccotti, so it was stale and useless by the time it reached my newsroom. The second explanation is that, according to my editors, the draft was even less insightful than the series I once ran about the rat problem in Boston's collegiate underworld. Still I stand by this new-and-improved version, which I've remixed to emphasize my contempt for Manhattan's soulless Upper East Side, and to juxtapose the area's yuppie dipshit residents with Occupiers who disavow activist stereotypes. My original idea – to cause some ruckus with a crew of drunken anarchists – didn't pan out as planned. But as was the case with most attempts to document Occupy, I wound up with much more than just an awful hangover.

Up until now, the few beer summits I've had with Occupy Wall Street characters have been at Blarney Stone on Trinity Place. It's a worthy hole, with low ceilings and mismatched tiles, relatively cheap pours and, on most nights, a gaggle of friendly and talkative activists. I've even scored some minor tips there; over a barrage of shots in October, a leathery percussionist named Zeke schooled me on the simmering showdown between drummers and increasingly deaf campers that would soon reach a boiling point.

But at this juncture, nearly two months into the occupation, the Stone is a shitty place to discuss the movement. Hanging there is hardly different from chilling at Zuccotti – on wet evenings the place even has the same cardboard stench – and most Occupiers won't open up to reporters in front of their comrades. My goal on this outing was to get heavily involved activists – many of whom are currently avoiding the media – to join me for a roundtable chat about OWS progress, and to tell me about their everyday routines. So I took two cab-loads of them as far away from Zuccotti as conceivably possible.

I made plans ahead of time to meet Becky – a 25-year-old Mainer who pilgrimaged to Occupy Wall Street on day one – near the food tent at midnight on Saturday. She and some of her camp friends agreed to join me on a field trip and blind-date interview orgy to the Upper East Side, where I've always found the bar scene to be a decadent playground populated by obnoxious post-collegiate dickheads. I figured that some bar up there – among finance types who yell "Get a job!" at protesters – would be an ideally ironic setting to discuss the Occupy grind.

I also hoped to stir drama. Not so much that we got assaulted by frat boys, but I at least thought someone in a pea coat would spit at us. That's my expectation of people who hang on the Upper East Side, where, in the wake of neocon outrage over France's not helping bomb Iraq, restaurants put signs in their windows assuring, WE DO NOT SELL FRENCH WINE. My experiment, however, didn't yield projectile saliva or douchebag yuppie behavior. If that wasn't shocking enough, my Zuccotti drinking pals weren't dirtbag drunks, as so many radio yappers would have you believe. Rather they're dedicated wonks who needed to get up early the next day and work.

BEHIND ENEMY LINES

We pick BB&R on Second Avenue for one reason: the bouncer says there's room for us out back. Though somewhat upscale with its chic onyx bar, the place essentially resembles every Upper East Side joint I ever drank at – pool table in the rear, hot bartenders with big balloons, the best of the '80s, '90s, and today blaring from a digital jukebox. Inside, some high-gloss brunettes are grinding to Ton Loc, while their guy friends pound shots and race their glasses to the table. Eric, an Indiana native and musician who joined Occupy last month, turns to me: "You have no idea how out of my element I am right now."

But I do have an idea – that's why we came here – and so do some cats who begin eyeballing us. No one is ice-grilling, but there's certainly an intrigue over Becky. With her whiffle cut and kaleidoscopic threads, she's the most colorful character in this sea of black-and-blue monotony. Her friend Stefan is also getting stared at; the Brooklynite-by-way-of-Baltimore is the only one in here with what could be described as a textbook Occupy uniform: haywire beard, flannel shirt, neck bandana, and a 'do that clearly wasn't messed on purpose.

A few humorless couples dressed in all-black, visibly disturbed by our snagging seats near them, bounce before we finish our first round. Works for us; we declare that the bar is now occupied, and my guests flick approval fingers in the air. Now we're grooving – even Stefan, who is mostly staying sober during his "intense state of new growth" at Zuccotti, sips a lager. Still, they're all business, drinking slowly and talking about camp without my coaxing them. Eric, the Indiana native who always found time to get trashed as a touring psychedelic rocker, says revolution's the priority.

"I was closing down bars in Bloomington until the day I came to Wall Street," says Eric, who hitched a ride to New York last month after hearing that Zuccotti might get raided. Now he works 16-hour days in the food tent, where he recently helped implement a Google Voice-powered meal delivery system for off-site working groups. "Life as a touring musician was amazing, and there's no doubt that I partied hard, but everything I've done here is so fulfilling that I don't even miss it."

LAST CALL
After several rounds the group is still talking about work, and Wall Street indiscretions – even after I joke that they don't have to impress me. Stefan and Becky are discussing nonviolent planning, and analyzing the pros and cons of "spokescouncil" models for consensus building. We're joined by Lori, a college student from Kentucky who, with her chopped bangs and fashionably tight dress, could easily blend with the native set. Lori flew into New York last month to see friends; but after visiting Zuccotti, she wound up putting school on hold and camping out full time.

In the moment, I'm fascinated by their dedication. With pressing issues to address like camp winterization, the Occupiers hardly acknowledge the flatscreens flashing above them. Max, a bespectacled Brown grad with a teaching background, tells me that he's just too busy for things like sports and television: "If you don't show up at a normal job, they can usually get by without you," he says. "But with us, if you don't show up, all sorts of balls get dropped. At Zuccotti, I've learned a level of commitment and responsibility that's way higher than anything I've learned from other things I've done before."

Their constant obligations aside, the gang assures me that tonight is the perfect time for this adventure. Camp is more relaxed now than it's ever been, with everyone focusing on headline-grabbing actions to commemorate the two-month anniversary of Occupy in five days. I ask them if plans include a romp on the Upper East Side, perhaps to remind young professionals that they're also part of the 99 percent. Becky says it's unlikely.

By 3am, they're all itching to leave. Eric thanks me for the beers but claims, "Zuccotti doesn't rest on Sundays," and says he has to make a meeting in five hours. I offer to buy one last round, but my photographer's the only taker; everyone else says the thought of working morning tasks hungover is too daunting. "I think I'm all done here," says Max. "But do you think they'd mind if I brush my teeth in the bathroom?"

THE COLD WAR

Originally published in:
The Boston Phoenix, November 16, 2011

More than almost anything else in this book, "The Cold War" reflects the non-stop hustle of covering Occupy – sleepless nights, chafed thighs, sudden and dramatic plot twists. The big, bad November raid on Zuccotti happened in the wee hours of a Tuesday, while longer *Phoenix* features are generally passed in on Monday at the latest. But the Wall Street eviction was huge news, and we all felt that it deserved a proper treatment instead of just a blog post. Fortunately, hip-hop mogul Russell Simmons came through Boston that day, giving me a local hook and – to my delight – borrowing my Sox hat to wear while he engaged reporters. Between the rush and excitement, all I really remember is a nauseous feeling, and that I somehow got my story in by deadline before flying to Seattle three hours later.

As New York City police scrubbed Occupy Wall Street clean of its inhabitants and their belongings Tuesday morning, emotions ran high back in Boston. Dewey Square squatters watched the live stream from Zuccotti Park on laptops. When word hit the Web that the New York encampment was under attack, people shouted across Dewey that Boston was next.

"It really didn't help the anxiety level around here," said John Ford, an Occupy Boston librarian and ubiquitous camp presence. "Everyone was mic-checking impending doom."

Hub activists were already nervous about their own fate – for days, the Boston Police Department had tried to block attempts to prepare the camp for winter, keeping heavy-duty tents out of the square and impeding the will of Occupiers who plan to crash through ski season.

First, this past Sunday, a BPD officer told the driver of a visiting Wikileaks donation truck – on camera – that police searched the truck "because we were afraid that you might have contraband that we don't want in the camp – winter tents and insulation materials." Asked where that order came from, the officer stated, "My bosses."

Second, reps from the Occupy Boston Women's Caucus were stopped from bringing in a new weatherproof canopy. They were upset that their attempt to build a safe space for female Occupiers had been thwarted. But the implication was more sinister. A BPD spokesperson confirmed to the *Phoenix*: "We are not allowing for anything that requires building materials."

It's clear that BPD doesn't expect the encampment to last the winter – and they're not eager to make it any easier for them. This is a national trend, as Boston and New York aren't the only cities that would be thrilled to see the last of the Occupiers. Hours after the Zuccotti raid, a video clip surfaced of Oakland Mayor Jean Quan – a notorious symbol of Occupy intolerance – telling the BBC that she had been conferencing with 18 other cities about how to handle their Occupy "situation."

IN TENTS

Many protesters at Occupy Wall Street have long speculated that Mayor Michael Bloomberg and his cronies want to wipe out Occupy before the cold comes – or at least make Occupiers vulnerable to foul weather. This was apparent to them from the early days of the movement, when police removed tents and tarps on sight. In fact, Zuccotti only became a tent city after October 17, when cops threatening to dismantle the sheltered medical area stood down to the Rev. Jesse Jackson. Within hours, tents were planted throughout the park, but many still thought that it was only a matter of time before cops leveled the encampment.

That's why Zuccotti organizers took advantage of a lull this past weekend to prep for the future. Members of the "Town Planning" working group told the *Phoenix* that their first agenda item was winterization – figuring ways to replace store-bought tents with more resilient military-grade numbers. On top of that, they were also hatching major actions for a two-month anniversary bash. Operatives would not disclose exactly what sort of peaceful pandemonium might transpire – other than the publicized promise to "shut down Wall Street" – but all agreed that Thursday would bring the biggest demonstrations yet, a spectacle sure to rally new support and re-energize participants.

For all their plotting, though, Occupiers had no clue what was in store. Shortly after 1am on Tuesday morning, hundreds of New York City law enforcement officers surrounded the park's perimeter, blocked (and in some cases even arrested) credentialed and alternative media, and cuffed about 200 protesters – 142 inside the park, and the rest while they were fleeing through surrounding streets.

The effects were as expected – in less than 24 hours, tens if not hundreds of thousands of Occupiers worldwide were marching in solidarity with their Zuccotti brothers and sisters. In Boston, more than 300 chanted through the streets: "NEW YORK IS BOSTON – AND BOSTON IS NEW YORK."

RUSH HOUR
Occupy Boston was quiet in the wake of the Zuccotti raid – many Occupiers had stayed up past 4am watching the live stream from New York, and were sleeping in when local media swarmed Dewey for reactions during rush hour. But everyone was up by 11am, with a small group off to lobby at the State House, some giving TV interviews, and most waiting on legendary hip-hop mogul and progressive activist Russell Simmons. Word on Twitter was that Simmons planned to deliver a major announcement, and perhaps even some hope after the bulldozing that transpired in Zuccotti.

Sure enough, Simmons arrived at Dewey just after noon, brandishing a single piece of paper. "This is a proposed constitutional amendment drafted by one of the most senior members of the United States Senate," said Simmons. He went on to read the anonymously scribed measure, which would make all presidential and congressional campaigns publicly financed, and prohibit federal candidates from accepting outside contributions. "This simple constitutional amendment makes all the difference in the world," said Simmons, who added that the amending process will commence as soon as the Democratic senator who drafted the proposal finds a Republican co-sponsor.

Even as Simmons was addressing Dewey, legal advocates for Occupy Boston were handling a more imminent concern, filing a lawsuit in Suffolk Superior Court to prevent their own eviction. They'd been considering such legal maneuvers for days, but were finally spurred into action by the OWS pillage. There would not be a decision until later in the week – a hearing was scheduled for Wednesday morning – but until then, activists found some assurance in news from New York, where a judge ruled that protesters could remain in Zuccotti (though without tents).

"It was horrifying to see what happened on Wall Street last night," said Ford, the camp librarian. "I'll tell you one thing, though – if they're going to lie in the road and get in the way of our peaceful progress, then we're ready for whatever they've got."

November 06 | Day 51

Meet Tim from Tampa
Occupier and fireman
Jailed for protesting

November 07 | Day 52

Occupy Tuscon
Sleeper movement of the pack
Refuse to leave park

November 08 | Day 53

It's election day
Occupy the voting booth
Not such a success

November 09 | Day 54

Thirty-nine arrests
Cal Berkeley lights the fire
Campus police roar

November 10 | Day 55

Harvard occupied
Most exclusive in nation
Guards keep public out

November 11 | Day 56

Eleven three times
Historic date so why not
Occupy the world

November 12 | Day 57

Time to hit Brooklyn
Borough Hall to Borough Park
Speak-outs and teach-ins

November 13 | Day 58

Occupy Portland
Cleared out after tense stand-off
Ugliness follows

November 14 | Day 59

Occupy Oakland
Camp pillaged by Mayor Quan
Cabinet crumbles

November 15 | Day 60

Raid on Zuccotti
End of encampment era
Disrespect books crushed

WILD WILD WEST COAST

Originally published in:
The Boston Phoenix, November 23, 2011

Seattle was the first occupied city I encountered where trained media professionals – even TV guys in suits and ties – marched with eye-rinsing solution just in case police attacked them. It wouldn't be the last time I saw that, as a reporter friend in Oakland had a bandana wrapped around his mug on account of a cop there who, weeks earlier, shot rubber bullets at a photog. The West Coast was insane, and I would have loved to pound the Pacific for months, stomping over bridges and chronicling massive port shutdowns. But I had less than a week to take it all in, digest the sights, and write a feature. I was a degenerate one-man stampede if there ever was one, but I pulled it off thanks to fistfuls of chemically cocked chronic, face-bending boomers, and ecstatic Occupy energy from Seattle to the Bay.

Whether true or not, it's always been my vague impression that West Coasters take as much pride in relaxation as East Coasters do in being assholes. On trips to California, friends yell at me for walking too fast. In Los Angeles, I constantly scream on slowpokes in parking lots and café lines. Spicoli. *Portlandia.* Too $hort. The Beach Boys. The Pacific states, I thought, were chill.

So since Occupy began, I've been surprised to see such extreme brutality unfold out West, from San Diego to Seattle. The situation in Oakland struck me as particularly alarming, even though I'm well aware of the ongoing tumult there since a transit cop shot and killed unarmed 22-year-old Oscar Grant on a train platform three years ago. Tainted history or not, the images of Oakland officers indiscriminately shooting tear gas and rubber bullets at peaceful protesters were significantly more barbaric than anything I'd witnessed at Occupy demonstrations back East.

After months of communicating with contacts in Seattle and Oakland, last week I went to see the savagery for myself, and to check out these Occupy camps that have been crushed by recent police raids. Things got even worse during the course of my expedition, as videos went viral of University of California-Davis campus cops deploying projectile chemicals as if they were watering a lawn.

After nearly a week on the ground – riding trains and planes down the coast – it's clear to me that authorities have escalated manageable situations into constant chaos. I've also seen that they never learn from their mistakes, continuing to anoint memes, mascots, and martyrs like Dorli Rainey, the 84-year-old Seattle woman who cops blasted with pepper spray just hours before I touched down.

SEATTLE

WEDNESDAY

The general assembly is entering its second hour of a hot discussion about what defines violence. I've seen this issue raised at nearly all of the Occupied cities that I've been to, and it goes the same here as it has everywhere else: soft-spoken women and effeminate men make their case for unconditional nonviolence, only to be overpowered by a charismatic anarchist in leather who pumps the crowd full of adrenaline. Tonight is especially contentious at Seattle's sprawling Capitol Hill encampment, since, on a march yesterday, cops sprayed a blind man, the Occupy Seattle chaplain, a pregnant 19-year-old, and Rainey, whose story is a source of international outrage by the time I arrive.

The miserable weather couldn't be more cliché if it was raining lattes. Still, despite the nonstop drizzle, camp is jumping, with a long and anxious queue to speak at GA, and people hanging late afterward to discuss planned actions for the two-month anniversary of Occupy Wall Street the next day. Cornel West charged their batteries with a speech earlier this afternoon, and a few people are determined to take back their second camp in the bourgeois Westlake shopping district. Occupiers have been forcibly removed from there four times, most recently yesterday, when many – including Rainey – were peppered and six were arrested.

Home base is on the skirt of the Seattle Central Community College campus, and has one of the most magnificent waterproof set-ups I've seen at any Occupy. It's clean, has respectable Porta Potties, and even features a three-level structure that houses more than a dozen people. Since they're not permitted to have nails, camp architects researched building methods that entail just wood and rope. The result is a labyrinthine fort enclosed in plastic and tapestries that any kid would kill to play in, and that Occupy Seattle's roughly 300 full-time residents use for everything from meetings to sign-making. A homeless guy named David takes me inside, and an inviting group of artists fills me in on yesterday's attacks. They offer to put me up in the solarium for the night, and while their lair is much nicer than my accommodations, I graciously decline and retreat back to my motel.

THURSDAY
By morning, Seattle Mayor Mike McGinn has formally apologized to Rainey for any inconvenience that the police chemical bath may have caused the octogenarian. But that didn't calm people at Community College, where guys in sleeveless denim coats with fist patches are soaking bandanas in a mix of orange juice and vinegar – just in case their eyes get stung again during today's march. All morning, television news stations were reporting that Occupy protests are going to impede traffic, and the squad brewing here at 3pm is going to make sure of that. As soon as about 100 students from the college march out of their building behind an SCCC IS OCCUPIED banner, the rest fall in line and head north toward the University of Washington.

They've been here before; on November 2, about 300 of them picketed a speech that JP Morgan Chase CEO Jamie Dimon was giving to the university's business students. Still, despite mass arrests during that dust-up, both Occupiers and labor organizers are determined to lean on the massive state school, which still hasn't pledged support for the movement. After the first two miles, wrapping around lakes and under bridges, it's clear that some shit's about to go down, whether peaceful or not. They're moving faster, chanting things like, "They say, 'Cutbacks' – We say, 'Fuck that.'" The rain is torrential; still, nobody seems fazed – including the Livestream videographer who's in a full-body winter suit, shielding his Saran-wrapped laptop with an umbrella. And then we hit the University Bridge, where more than 3000 union teachers, laborers, and members of their families walk south and meet us. It's a streamlined operation – workers in orange vests and SEIU hats guide the horde, and everybody heeds. Though there were some cops on the march – including one on a motorcycle who twice plowed through the crowd, and a few in riot gear along the way – police back off by several hundred yards once the bridge is taken. After two hours, during which Occupiers scale trestles and condemn Republican students from the University of Washington, the crowd disperses without a fight. Their message, one student speaker shouts while hammering a fist at his own campus below, is the same that Occupiers delivered to downtown Seattle two days prior, when police made Rainey a household name: "If you're not with us – then you're against us."

PORTLAND

FRIDAY

Authorities in Portland have been playing whack-a-mole with Occupiers for a week now. After Mayor Sam Adams warned that on November 13 he'd shut down two settled camps – located across the street from one another in downtown Portland – police went in two days early, beginning a tense and prolonged showdown leading up to the planned eviction. When clean-up cops – dressed in riot gear, gripping fistfuls of pepper spray – finally came to Chapman and Lownsdale squares on the 13th, the ensuing clash resulted in 51 arrests, a public transportation shutdown, and the dislocation of several hundred Occupiers, many of whom had been there since October 6.

Following that wipeout, many Occupiers shacked up with friends in nearby college dorms and apartments, some of which are still sleeping more than 15 to a living room. They've also gotten love from local churches, which continue to provide food, meeting space, and even shelter. All prior communications with municipal authorities were severed after the raid, leaving hundreds of Occupiers indefinitely homeless, but not undetermined. A rogue bunch tried to hold down Terry Schrunk Plaza – a federal space near the two city parks that got scrubbed – but couldn't stay for long. The week before, on Guy Fawkes Day, 10 were jailed after chaining themselves to a cement-filled drum in the plaza and refusing to leave.

I arrive in Portland on a damp and dreary afternoon and find a half-dozen Occupy organizers meeting with young labor leaders at the First Unitarian Church. It's an intimate engagement, so I announce myself, and they agree to let me listen in. They mostly talk tactics and about actions coming up on Sunday. Specifically, the Occupy representatives are preparing for an event called "Meet the Occupation," in which union workers, their families, and other community members can come and see that Occupiers don't bite. Due to several televised spats with the law, and some of the laziest news coverage of Occupy that I've seen clean across the country, their image has suffered among Oregonians. This team hopes to fix what might be the movement's worst PR problem anywhere.

Two blocks away, at 7pm, I find the rest of the nomads inside the First Congregationalist Church, where about a dozen gentle-hearted parishioners are accommodating Occupiers with ramen noodles, coffee, and a space for their weekly spokescouncil – an all-encompassing meeting in which one delegate from each working group presents progress updates. In a magnificent hall on the second floor, about 200 people – bearded old-school long-hairs, a tattooed lumberjack in a wife beater, several hipsters dressed like Pippi Longstocking – listen attentively as facilitators recap the past few days of setbacks, then disperse the bunch into breakout sessions to engage business on everything from shelter to upcoming Black Friday actions.

Meanwhile, downstairs in the church basement, I meet some kind twentysomethings in spike-clad coats and cut-off gloves who are sitting with all of their possessions packed in duct-taped bags by their feet. They tell me they don't have much left since their eviction from camp; Carmen, a 25-year-old who moved here three years ago from North Dakota, says she's out a blanket, shoes, tent, tarp, and clothes.

After we hang for a bit Carmen also says that her street friends – affectionately known as "the concrete kids" – believe that their puppy Chubbs was bulldozed along with all the gear. As she's saying this outside over a cigarette, I hear screams of joy and see a mob swarm around a young woman. It's Liz Nichols, their friend who'd overnight become a national Occupy icon for a picture of her swallowing a mouthful of pepper spray. I wait for things to calm down, make my way toward her, and stupidly ask how she's doing.

Says Nichols: "Considering that I was pepper-sprayed, that I can't find any of my stuff, and that I just found out that the abandoned house we've been crashing in was raided by cops overnight while I was in jail – I'd say that I'm doing pretty good."

OAKLAND

SATURDAY

Nationally publicized police brutality has hardly done wonders for Oakland's tourism industry. For just 40 bucks on Priceline, I booked a room at the Marriott Courtyard – only a block away from City Hall, where Occupiers camped up until November 14, and near where cops fractured the skull of former Marine Scott Olsen in late October.

Videos of Olsen being pelted with tear gas canisters were among the first visuals to spur a national discussion about the inhumane treatment of Occupy protesters, and Oakland activists also got another sympathy boost when Deputy Mayor Sharon Cornu – and Mayor Jean Quan's chief legal advisor, Dan Siegel – resigned after the November crackdown.

When I arrive at Frank Ogawa Plaza – renamed Oscar Grant Plaza by Occupiers in memory of the 22-year-old killed by a BART transit cop in 2009 – thousands of people are gathered around the giant quad in front of Oakland City Hall. Most avoid the grassy parts, though, since the city intentionally flooded them in a successful attempt to keep Occupiers out. Nevertheless, they're showing up 10, 20, and even 50 at a time – the National Union of Healthcare Workers, masked Web hacktivists, Black Panthers, extended families, and hundreds of Oakland teachers, who are rallying to stop five school closings.

After a half-hour of drums, poetry, and impassioned rants about banks and inequality, they're off, stretching across more than five blocks by the time all of the platoons line up. The celebration doesn't stop when the march begins, though; there are at least half-a-dozen dance parties along the route, including one around a brass band and another on a flatbed truck fueled by fitting anthems like "Sound of Da Police."

Most people are packing some sort of mask or bandana and a plastic bag with anti-pepper-spray solution, but there's hardly a police presence on today's march. I ask around about why there are only a few cops in sight – some with signs on their back that say NEGOTIATOR – and am told that, while things are cool now, they're bound to heat up later when the group tries to squat in a new lot five blocks from City Hall (as proof they point to the three or four helicopters hovering above). Before that encore, though, the march pauses to rally outside a school facing imminent closure. There, above the crowd on one side of the Grand Lake cinema, is a sign advertising the new biopic *J. Edgar* – signaling more than a few cracks about how the former FBI chief is posthumously monitoring radicals. On the other side of the overhang is a short poem in backlit letters: "No one can evict an idea whose time has come. Shame on you Mayor Quan."

When we get to the corner of Telegraph Avenue and 19th Street – the site of a fenced-in abandoned lot that Occupiers planned to commandeer – I expect nothing less than a fully loaded riot squad. But the 30-or-so cops standing across the street and around the perimeter have no masks or helmets on. Furthermore, they don't even flinch as mobs of rabid Occupiers unravel hundreds of feet of chain links, push through gates, and run through the lot cheering. When resourceful Occupiers begin constructing a tent-and-tarp city using sticks and pipes from the massacred fences, police still leave them alone for more than two hours, until 10pm, when authorities instruct the driver of the aforementioned flatbed truck, which is still fueling a dance party, to vacate. He does, but gets pulled over blocks away.

After a stand-off with about 20 cops, one officer enters the party truck and drives off, telling the nonviolent but verbally aggressive crowd that the vehicle will be impounded for 30 days. But while two protesters claim to be sideswiped by an unmarked cruiser fleeing the scene (and show everyone their bruises to prove it), the situation de-escalates as quickly as it started. Everyone heads back to the newly occupied lot, where there are about 100 people left with some others crashed in tents. Some seem wary about how long they'll last here, but they still mark the day a victory.

SUNDAY
When I return the next morning, the tents are down, the tarps are gone. I see a young hippie couple that I met the night before, and the dreadlocked girl tells me they were raided at 8am, and

that, after some shouting, everyone decided to go peacefully. "We'll be back," she tells me. "Whether it's here or somewhere else." I look around, and there's no real trace of last night's action besides a pile of fencing. Across the street, discarded on a curb, I find one of the many doctored signs that Occupiers hung around the lot hours earlier: PIGS GO HOME. NO TRESPASSING WITHOUT WRITTEN PERMISSION OF OCCUPANTS!!! PURSUANT TO THE POWER OF THE PEOPLE.

SILENT PARTNERS

Originally published in:
The Boston Phoenix, November 30, 2011

I've always hated cops. As a teen, I was arrested several times for everything from disturbing the peace to criminal conspiracy, the latter of which stemmed from a fake ID operation that got me expelled from college. Later, as a reporter, I began impugning the Boston Police Department for questionable tactics; in 2010, for example, a swarm of cops kicked the snot out of an unarmed teenager in public – and got away with it. Yet in standing on the front lines of Occupy, I came to believe that they're not all savages. It's easy to wrap pigs in blanket statements, since at the core of their job is a commitment to defend a flawed system and its evil benefactors. But while officers who battered Occupiers will be banished to history's dunce corner with Klansmen and Confederates, it's important to acknowledge the few good men among the goons.

As Occupy camps from coast to coast face evictions – and in many cases have already been pushed out of parks and plazas like so much human trash – it's clear that the institutional response to the movement is escalating dangerously. Likewise, relations between police and activists seem to be deteriorating, as non-violent protesters continue to be arrested almost daily.

But as tensions build between Occupiers and Big Brother, what's also true is that individual officers are increasingly concerned about their role in combating Occupy. Even in cities where the overall police response has been barbaric, there's a growing sense that cops who've been charged with breaking camps are unnerved by such orders.

Earlier this week, Los Angeles authorities avoided a riot by working with protesters, and even thanking them publicly for demonstrating their right to free speech. On a smaller scale, last month in Oregon an officer was seen sobbing in his combat gear while raiding a Portland encampment. In October, Albany police – along with state troopers – refused to arrest protesters despite pressure from the city's mayor and New York Governor Andrew Cuomo.

At least one Occupier believes that such sentiments are not anomalous. Calling himself Danny – he wouldn't reveal his true identity – he created a movement-within-a-movement, Occupy Police (OcPo), designed to be an outlet for officers of all ranks, everywhere, to speak openly about Occupy.

"We think solidarity with police is needed," says Danny in the only interview he's granted to date. As he launches Operation SHIELD – an OcPo initiative calling for civilians, ex-police, and ex-military to physically step in between protesters and cops in the event of future confrontations – Danny's goal is to bridge this most glaring divide among so-called 99 percenters. He continues: "There are a lot of active cops right now who can't speak, can't get involved, and have no place in this protest . . . but they sympathize with the direction of the movement and its political standpoints – that the system is screwed up, and that this is about bad government. They also believe that it's not good for this to turn into a street war between police and protesters."

UNHAPPY OFF THE RECORD
Danny started OcPo in mid-October, after a series of intense talks with buddies on the Boston force about the eviction of Occupiers from the Rose Kennedy Greenway on Columbus Day. "My friends who are cops did not like what happened," he says. "They have to do their job – and they can't act out about it openly – but they're unhappy off the record with what's going on, and they're not happy with having to arrest non-violent protesters."

By early November, OcPo had thousands of connections on Facebook and Twitter, and what Danny described as an outpouring of moral support and gratitude from police. While any cop who supports OcPo understandably can't say so in public (or to the *Phoenix*), the platform has allowed at least one officer to express himself. Fred Shavies of Oakland PD was accused by activists of attempting to covertly infiltrate the Occupy in his city. "I totally agree with Occupy Wall Street," Shavies says in a video on the OcPo Web site. "I identify with the 99 percent, but I also have a job to do."

Danny says OcPo's mission is to give men and women like Shavies "a place to speak, and to create peace and solidarity between the two groups so they can combine and make real political change." For proof that those ideas have gained traction, he points to one of the Occupy movement's defining moments: the November 17 arrest of former Philadelphia police captain Ray Lewis. Retired for eight years and living in the Catskills, on November 14 –

after weeks of reading about people who were standing up to corporate entities that he too deplores – Lewis became inspired to join forces with OWS protesters.

The arrest of Lewis, on the two-month anniversary of Occupy Wall Street, hit the press like a billy club. Though more than 300 were bagged by NYPD on the same day, the images of him being cuffed in full police uniform – and news of his being subsequently slapped with charges including disorderly conduct – put Lewis front and center. With the world watching, he showed compassion for fellow men and women of the law. "Corporate America is using police departments as hired thugs," Lewis told MSNBC. "I was trying to portray the message that they should not become mercenaries – not that they already were. . . . Cops are just as human as everyone else."

'A HUGE STATEMENT'
With more and more examples of police benevolence to counter the tragedies that have unfolded in their clashes with Occupiers, Danny's latest push is to bring OcPo off the Web and onto the front lines. With Operation SHIELD, he's collaborating with the similarly themed Occupy Marine Corps (OMC) to recruit "an organized and very transparent group of men and women who will have the guts to step up in between the protesters and the police and create a gridlock." Logistics are still being drawn up, but Danny believes that his growing networks can support such interrupter actions.

According to Todd Gitlin, an author, Columbia professor, and veteran activist who has closely watched social movements – including Occupy Wall Street – over the past several decades, Operation SHIELD is a historically unique concept. But while "police were the hardest nut to crack in the late '60s and '70s," Gitlin says the impact of servicemen and women speaking out against wars has always been powerful. "Whenever somebody acts out of the character imputed to them, it's a huge statement," he says. "What it did for the morale of the [anti-war] movement was assure people that they were not wholly isolated, and that theirs is not just a matter of piety or moral righteousness – that it was a reasonable position that reasonable people could sign up for."

Recent examples all across the country have so far proven that such phenomena endure. When police raided Occupy Boston, the prevalent emerging image was that of a member of the group Veterans for Peace being arrested while his American flag was trampled. In Oakland, outrage ensued following reports that Iraq War veteran Scott Olsen was assaulted with a can of tear gas. In building Operation SHIELD, Danny has connected with all of these emblematic entities, including Marine Corps Sergeant Shamar Thomas. A hulking presence, Thomas, an Iraq War vet, famously blocked NYPD from arresting protesters during a march into Times Square on October 15. In the moment, Shamar expressed what could be considered the rallying sentiment behind OcPo and Operation SHIELD.

"It is not honorable to attack unarmed civilians who carry no weapons, who have no intent or ability to harm you," the veteran told more than 30 police officers – and subsequently the whole world, as video of his declaration went viral hours later. "It is not honorable to suppress the right to freedom of speech and freedom of association. You carry your badges and your guns and your authority because you are charged with protecting the innocent. We are the innocent. You are working for the criminals."

November 16 | Day 61

B of A protests
San Fran doesn't fuck around
Hundred cuffed and stuffed

November 17 | Day 62

Anniversary
Two months of revolution
Can't knock the hustle

November 18 | Day 63

UC-Davis scene
Casual pepper-spraying
Meet Lieutenant Pike

November 19 | Day 64

Sixty-four days passed
Four-thousand jailed nationwide
Moving right along

November 20 | Day 65

Albany cops chill
Ignore Cuomo 'til this point
Forty-eight arrests

November 21 | Day 66

Fox News strikes again
Megyn Kelly on Bill-O
Pepper spray veggies

November 22 | Day 67

Obama stumping
But mic checked in New Hampshire
Primary preview

November 23 | Day 68

Fifty officers
Arrest ten in Charleston raid
Five punks for each perp

November 24 | Day 69

Happy Thanksgiving
Just don't try feeding people
Good will is outlawed

November 25 | Day 70

Fuck Black Friday buzz
Occupiers take to streets
Give free shit away

OCCUPY THE HOOD II CHICAGO

Unpublished:
December 2, 2011

I spent the three days leading up to the 2008 presidential election on the South Side of Chicago. It was the most impoverished hellhole that I'd ever seen, the only place where someone, concerned about my safety, ever stopped their car to ask if my caucasian ass needed a ride home. In my line of work I've seen a lot of ghettos, but Chicago's crack torch despair moved me to tears, as one black resident after another told me that their situations were dire, and that they didn't think that their beloved senator becoming president would change that. Exactly three years later, after hanging for a few nights with the general assembly in ice cold Grant Park, I directed my attention to the poor and dangerous 'hoods outside the downtown Loop. Things had changed. They'd gotten worse.

The curbside afternoon assembly that broke me into Occupy Chicago was not raucous. None of the dozen-or-so participants gave announcements, nor did anybody seize the soapbox and preach to passing finance chumps on lunch break. Despite the tranquility, though, after just a few minutes two cops moved toward Tony, a dedicated Occupier who sleeps on this corner in the Financial District most nights, and who was facilitating the gathering. Tony saw what was coming and called it quits, telling everyone that business would resume later in Grant Park. Familiar with the drill, he then grabbed his cartful of signs, and began to walk up and down the block. "They say that we can't stand still," he told me. "We have to move 15 feet in one direction, then 15 feet in another. It's ridiculous."

Back in Boston, some Occupiers were considering plans to vacate Dewey Square on their own terms. I flew to Chicago to impugn the camp-less movement there, hoping to get a glimpse of what might be next in cities where Occupy is fast-becoming a nomadic enterprise. Windy City Occupiers never even got a chance to plant their flag. Efforts to settle in Grant Park were met with titanic police resistance. The rumor was that Mayor Rahm Emmanuel didn't want protesters getting ideas for May 2012, when Chicago will host the G8 and NATO summits – both of which have a 99 percent likelihood of being enthusiastically picketed.

The cold treatment of Occupiers downtown hobbled the Chicago outpost from early on. It also gave birth to a number of active local Occupy the Hood fronts, which were rising from the ashes of oppressed communities across the country. So despite meeting many pleasant people on my first night in Grant Park, I spent the rest of my time in Chicago on the South Side, where an overwhelming number of the city's 100,000 foreclosed homes mar the already blighted landscape. There I met troops who were opening new theaters in a war that many gave up fighting years ago. One of them was New Beginnings Church pastor Corey Brooks, who, inspired by Occupy, moved into a tent on the roof of an abandoned hotel across the street from his church.

I heard the mayor visited you up here.

The mayor didn't visit, but his staff came and asked questions about what I'd like the city to do. The mayor called, but while he was excited that someone was speaking out against violence, he wasn't so excited about me being on top of a vacant building.

Tell me about your church.

Our church is 11 years old, and we've been in the building [across the street] for four to five years. It was an old dilapidated skating rink and we went in and gutted it ourselves. We had the sanctuary done by a contractor but all the rest of the building we did on our own.

How much did you raise and how did you go about that?

We secured a loan from a bank for $4.5 million.

A local bank?

Yes, but we realize now that we'd never do that again because the debt kills you. Now we've taken on a theme of not being in debt anymore – it really limits everything we're trying to do, and when you have limited resources already, it just compounds the situation.

Your church has things like a school, a community center, and an exercise room. How desperately needed were these things around here?

We wanted more than just a church – we wanted a church that reaches a community. You can't just have a building and only come together on Sunday without offering other things. We started looking at what we need – like health. We have all these health issues, so let's put together a gym so we can get these guys and these ladies in here to exercise. Then there's education, so we started a school that goes from kindergarten through eighth grade.

But this motel that we're on top of now was right across the street. How problematic was it when they were still open?

The building had a lot of prostitution – this was known as the prostitution strip, so if you wanted a prostitute, you came to this little field, you came to this little strip, and you got a prostitute. That's a well-known fact. Outside of that, there was a lot of drug use, and a lot of drug sales, and just a lot of crime in general.

When did it close down?

It's been closed for about a year-and-a-half now.

Did it get worse?

When it first closed you could see an immediate change – there'd be no prostitutes, and for a minute there were no drug dealers, like they'd been completely wiped out. The only thing they didn't do was a good job of boarding it up, and because of that people were able to get in. Some people were living here, others were stealing pipes and copper and anything else they could scrap to buy drugs. From there, you had rooms with people going in and out for crack. Basically, it just became a whole different type of problem, so our church secured it and boarded it up ourselves.

Who owns it now?

There are two banks along with a guy who lives in India, and who signed his rights over to the bank that I'm negotiating with. Basically our contract is that we have it in escrow right now, and we have to raise a whole lot of money to get control of it.

If you don't leave this tent, how do you speak to your congregation?

I don't do the services. I don't even leave this tent or really go on the roof except to exercise out back. I don't go down to my church though; we stream live on Sundays, so when I preach, I'll be sitting in a chair up here speaking into a camera.

So is it fair to say that you're an Occupier?

They reached out to me, and I appreciate it because I really do believe it's going to take people from outside of our community to help us resolve some of these issues. Our goal is to shine light on the issues so people outside the inner-city see that things are only getting worse here. But they have to be sensitive enough to understand that we have a vision, that we believe in what we're trying to do. We want to collaborate with [Occupy], but we want to do it so that we don't get in each other's way.

What will you do if you raise the money that you're hoping for?

We'll tear it down and build a structure that helps us combat educational issues, social issues, economic issues, and spiritual issues. We want it to be a community center with a gymnasium, a small theater, classrooms where we can do counseling, and a doctor's office so people can get free check-ups. As part of the way to pay for this, we want to build commercial spaces on the first floor, and hopefully bring in something like a Chipotle or Panera Bread. We need things like that here too.

Is this a food desert around here?

You bet it is. You have an inadequate grocery store with all generic brands at high prices, and no real chain store.

What other imminent problems do you face?

It's a couple of things. One is that we have so much violence in our neighborhood – that's one of the reasons that we're up here. From February to now there have been 10 black males 25-and-under that have been shot and killed around here. That's in a one-mile radius. We were recently burying a young man who was only 17. His parents were members of my church and kids from another area came and started to shoot at the church. These are really depraved actions. I do a lot of prison work behind the wall with real OGs, and even they say this stuff would have never happened 30 years ago. They have a thing now going on where they want to go to the funeral and shoot the body.

Excuse me?!?

It happened on the West Side so that's kind of like the thing. It's hard to believe, but we're dealing with a group of kids that lack any kind of education. Throw in the inability to get a job or to have money, and it's a bombshell waiting to explode. Add in hopelessness, and it's a really bad situation. We're trying to reach them, but it's hard because you're telling them that it's going to get better, and they're wondering how that could ever happen. The things they see on a day-to-day basis don't lead them to believe that. The Loop is only a half-a-mile from here, but you have kids who have never been there. They have no concept of what's going on downtown.

I heard that not too long ago you asked young men to hand over their weapons. What happened?

After that funeral, I said that I wanted any guns that were in the church to be left in the church. At first no one came forward, and then eventually one guy came forward, and then another guy, and then another guy. It ended up being four guns.

That must have been a pretty touching moment.

In a way it was a lesson. You can't complain about what people aren't doing for you. I believe that you have to be in the mindset that sometimes you have to do things for yourself. You can't just cry about a situation – you have to do something about it. I chose to take action.

SINK OR SWIM

Originally published in:
The Boston Phoenix, December 5, 2011

I wrote dozens of blog posts on the inner workings of Occupy Boston, most of which were left out of this project. Somehow I didn't feel that long accounts of free haircut day at Dewey Square – re-hashed six months after the fact – would resonate with readers outside of Massachusetts. But this screed stands out, as Boston Occupiers clashed with police during an attempt to bring a stainless steel sink into camp, and earned national attention as a result (they'd mastered the PR game by this point). Insignificant as the specific events may be, Boston's kitchen debacle is a great metaphor for the recurring Occupy joke of authorities claiming to attack protesters for their own "protection." The whole thing reminds me of what hippies used to say when warmongers charged that America was fighting for peace in Vietnam: beating activists, and saying that it's for their benefit. It's like fucking for chastity.

I woke up early last Friday in Chicago, where I was covering that city's Occupiers and their push to move into a rented space. It was an exciting week, as the night before there'd been a heated general assembly, as well as news that Mayor Rahm Emanuel had possibly cancelled an event because of threats that students affiliated with the movement might protest.

Despite those developments, I didn't see a single mention of Occupy Chicago on any Windy City newscast Friday morning. Instead, the activists who I'd been covering for months back in Boston had followed me to Illinois – and bogarted the cycle. Halfway through a buttered bagel, I looked up at the tube only to see familiar Dewey Square squatters clinging to a steel sink and chanting "Let us do the dishes!"

I wasn't totally surprised. I'd assumed that all eyes were already on Boston since the day before, when Occupiers began their anticipated court sashay with the city. Still this was a significant feat – in addition to network and cable buzz all around the country, the sink showdown went viral thanks to lifts from Daily Kos and *Wired*, among others. All this with minimal arrests, violence, and injuries.

From there something clicked with the often savvy, yet sometimes self-destructive Occupy Boston info disseminators. As demonstrated at their inclusive off-camp assembly in Copley Square this past Saturday – attended by dozens of newly interested Occupiers – Hub operatives are actively showcasing that they're not the dirty and disorganized Neanderthals that authorities have pegged them.

With the sink spat, Occupiers highlighted the irony in claims that their encampment is unsanitary; the powers-that-be say that Dewey Square is infested, yet won't let them improve conditions (they've also yet to cite them for health-related violations). Similarly, despite claims that the camp is combustible, they're not permitted to install new flame-retardant shelters.

Today, Occupiers gathered on the South Station side of Dewey for the arrival of a military tent the likes of which police have been instructed to keep out (along with any other building materials or so-called structures). This was no sneak job, like when their ninja unit smuggled in the current food tent two weeks ago. This was a PR job – announced days ahead of time.

Whereas the sink incident was a phenomenal lesson that evolved from a practical mission – to secure a dish-cleaning apparatus – the tent event was pure theater. Occupiers never intended to actually erect it or throw down with cops – they just wanted the press, whose attention they had after the sink story, to see first-hand how ridiculous police were being.

Beyond the symbolic cue of the tent, Occupy forces got an opportunity to debate inspectors and authorities in front of a crowd filled with reporters. On that front, protesters also delivered a decisive beat-down, as Boston is essentially arguing that while it was alright to bring tents in before, that is no longer the case. The city's insincere stance was cherry-topped with its suggestion that Occupiers secure permits from a municipal machine that wants them banished.

This campaign can't go on forever, as looming decisions in county court – and ultimately at City Hall – will dictate the fate of Dewey Square. There's also an outside chance that campers will dismantle things themselves and call it a win. But for the time being, there's no doubt about which side looks justified, and which is inventing rules on the fly.

November 26 | Day 71

LA camp deadline
City says it's last weekend
Protest says fat chance

November 27 | Day 72

Philly police chill
Most passive in the country
No prob past deadline

November 28 | Day 73

Coast to coast youth strike
Occupy the colleges
Cali to CUNY

November 29 | Day 74

Gas masks in LA
Busloads of cops head downtown
The crowd only grows

November 30 | Day 75

LA Doomsday looms
Eviction notice defied
Still hundreds of tents

December 01 | Day 76

Occupy Boston
In court defending Dewey
Encore with sink show

December 02 | Day 77

Nomadic Chi-town
Votes down proposed rental space
Too cold to twinkle

December 03 | Day 78

Copley Square rally
New attitude in the Bean
Big reach to public

December 04 | Day 79

NY farmers march
Fight over DC's wood fort
Or was it an ark

December 05 | Day 80

Murfreesboro beef
Titans want to set up tents
So much for 'free' claim

FACING EVICTION

Originally published in:
The Boston Phoenix, December 8-9, 2011

By this point I'd lost my mind. In reading this next chapter – a stew of three blog posts filed on the night of Dewey's false eviction alarm, and the day after Occupiers threw a huge dance party on Atlantic Avenue – it's important to acknowledge that little happening at this juncture had much to do with foreclosures, or wealth disparity, or golden parachutes. At the height of the war on Occupy Boston, I was as guilty as any number of other writers and activists who lost sight of the movement's underlying purpose. By the end, media coverage (including mine) was largely reduced to updates on legal battles and reports about petty clashes between cops and campers. With that said, while it was easy to lose focus when things got hectic, the most contentious situations were prime time to observe Occupiers in courageous moments.

STATEMENT FOR THE AGES
December 8, 2011 – 3pm

Occupiers are clearing tools out of the logistics and media hubs, unplugging cords and carting off their operations. The canopy of blue and green tarps atop Dewey Square is being dismantled, revealing bright tents that haven't seen sunlight in months. A bucket of butternut squash gets loaded into a van. So do the canned goods, which are headed to the Pine Street Inn. There are books from the Occupy Boston A to Z library boxed up everywhere, some free for the taking.

The Green Day working group has yet to blast "Time Of Your Life" over the speakers, but it's a last-day-of-high-school kind of feeling down here. People are mostly calm – with one notable exception in perpetual nuisance Phil, an out-of-work house painter who wears a kilt and likes to bark misogynistic threats at female campers. But there's a looming optimistic sadness for sure.

Not much was accomplished at today's emergency assembly, which followed the morning news that Occupiers have until midnight to vacate Dewey. Some vague announcements gave way to a vague arrangement for working groups to continue making plans on their own, with facilitators encouraging one and all to engage in creative autonomous actions.

As is not unusual, de facto spokespeople Alex Ingram and camp librarian John Ford blessed the press and crowd with some send-off bangers. Ingram dropped *Breakfast Club* knowledge, telling everyone that he'll remember them tomorrow – regardless of whether or not they wake up in the Square together. Ford then addressed, in a single sentence, what was on everybody's mind, asking people to think about "how much of a power play" it would be for the whole Occupation to pack up and vacate on their own terms.

It seems like a logistical impossibility to clear Dewey clean at this stage in the game. But they seem to be moving right along with the exodus. Tents are being dismantled, labeled, and stored for another day – whenever, wherever that may be. After nearly three months, it's beyond strange to watch.

In less than two hours, trucks are coming to cart away the media, spirituality, food, medic, library, and women's tents. In the rush, I was warmed to hear that some Occupiers are busy helping homeless people make arrangements for the coming weeks. Still there's a ton of work to be done. The food crew alone has been hauling crates and boxes for hours and is just now finishing up. Contrary to popular right-wing belief, a lot of Occupiers have day jobs, and they're not yet available to help the effort.

One supporter I spoke with said this whole thing reminds him of a governor's last day in office, when he or she triumphantly walks down the State House steps and enters the crowd, never to be seen again until returning as a lobbyist or presidential candidate. I'm not sure that's the right analogy, but I get what he's saying. As the longest-running Occupy camp in the country, Occupy Boston has a lot of eyes on it. To disappear before midnight, only to return in another place at another time, would be a statement for the ages. If they can pull it off.

THE FINAL COUNTDOWN
December 8, 2011 – 9pm

It's a mob scene at Occupy Boston tonight. A peaceful mob scene. The terrain is mostly muddy, with remnants of more than two months of 'round-the-clock revolution scattered over Dewey Square. The signs are packed up. So are most of the larger working group tents, including the enduring food operation, which now consists of just a table with some meager offerings. The only remaining perk is a crude bucketful of coffee that someone brought for the long haul.

As I'm filing this post, an assembly of several hundred is hashing out proposals for how Occupiers will handle tonight's looming, city-sponsored eviction. The seemingly prevailing game plan is billed as the "Dance Party" proposal, and will essentially call for the entire square to be cleared by midnight, at which time they'll boogie to celebrate evacuating on their own terms.

Whether or not that precise arrangement is stamped and approved, there are too many moving parts to squeeze tonight's proceedings into a single vote, or even into several. Some Occupiers are already refusing to move their tents, making it likely that police will forcibly evict them. There are also a number of rumors that, come midnight, a number of direct action-minded activists will unleash a torrent of creative non-violent resistance.

Police sources tell the *Phoenix* that while cops will certainly bring a significant presence tonight, they're not likely to actually raid (at least not in the nasty sense). They don't want a confrontation – especially now that they've seen Occupiers make efforts to clear out. Instead they reportedly plan to move in early – between last call and the morning news – sometime this weekend. That's hardly a surprise, of course, as such a move would minimize exposure to press and opposition.

As for the city line on this . . . Mayor Tom Menino said on radio earlier that he's "implementing the judge's orders." But according to the ruling regarding Dewey Square: "This decision clears the way but does not order the plaintiffs and other protesters to vacate the site." That's all legal smoke now though. There's not even an appeal filed, and if there was – Occupy Boston attorneys say it wouldn't change the reality that some hammers are about to swing down on the encampment.

At the time of this writing, there's less than two hours left – to the dance party, to the eviction, to the "Great Raid of 2011" – whatever you want to call it. They might do the Chicken Dance. They might do the Macarena. Word is they might take the party to the streets. Whatever Occupiers do though – whether it's group pandemonium or a concert of autonomous engagements – there's no doubt that there will be some fireworks this evening. Stay tuned.

THIS IS WHAT A BOILING POINT LOOKS LIKE
December 9, 2011 – 7pm

Dewey Square looks like a trampled battlefield today, with just a few dozen tents left among the planks, cardboard, packed boxes, and rubble. While the park-wide clean-up and vacate effort kicked off with a bang yesterday – allowing most Occupy Boston campers and working groups to safely store valuables – by this afternoon it had slowed to a crawl. Even those who were attempting to haul trash and goods seemed to be doing little more than moving rubbish from one side of Dewey to another.

At this point there's a strong sense that the end of this particular Dewey occupation – the longest running of its kind in the country at 70 days – is looming cold and hard. With that comes a general feeling – especially among those who physically remain – to stay put through the very end, until they're hauled off in city vehicles along with all their tents, flags, and other remnants of revolt. But what throws a giant wrench into their end game is the tactical advantage that police have. Right now in Dewey it's like *The Hills Have Eyes*. They're watching, and they're coming, but nobody knows quite when (though many believe the inevitable raid will come late tonight or late tomorrow night).

Things began to tense up at around 2pm today, when cops started shooing away people who were bringing food donations. The food tent as it once was is gone – a few folding tables in a puddle of vinegar mud remain, along with whatever scraps have been smuggled in – and authorities are ensuring that it stays that way. The same goes for just about everything else that folks have tried to bring – blankets, clothes, drinks. Clearly the mentality at police headquarters is that activists will be gone soon, so might as well make rank-and-file officers confront people over every slice of pizza that comes through the entrance.

To darken the mood, the Rose Kennedy Greenway Conservancy allegedly cut off power to the trapezoid for a few hours this afternoon. It's reportedly back on now, but the perceived symbolic "lights out" gesture was a real psychological bombshell. On top of that, some remaining Occupiers claim to have been told that Dewey will close at 11pm this evening. That could be a loose deadline like last night's vague threat, which resulted in little more than a rally dance party and two arrests. Or it could be the final kibosh. This is what a boiling point looks like.

DEWEY DECIMATED

Originally published in:
The Boston Phoenix, December 10, 2011

I thought about revamping this post from its original form. In the end, though, I decided to honor the mental state in which I wrote it. I'd just come home from the raid on Dewey, hadn't showered in days, and could smell my balls through my corduroys. My throat and lungs were burnt from choking on cold air and blunt smoke; my toes, wet and frigid, looked like day-old chicken nuggets. I'd agreed to be interviewed at noon by a reporter from *Columbia Journalism Review*, and, despite my condition, I didn't consider missing the appointment. We met near Dewey, which had already been wiped clean, and I was too exhausted to express much emotion (though I did manage to say "fuck" several times, on the record, in our interview). When we were done, I took an hour-long nap on a friend's couch, then bought a sweatshirt to keep warm, and headed to Boston Common for the first post-eviction assembly.

After more hours than I care to count I finally went to warm up in a press crash spot at around four in the morning. When I got back to Dewey Square 15 minutes later, a female member of the media team had been assaulted by a never-seen-before stranger in a dark suit. It was an extraordinarily strange occurrence by all accounts. The guy simply showed up, talked a bunch of shit, snatched a phone, slapped the camp Twitter pilot, and tried to run off before being arrested.

Whether this odd infiltration was deliberate or not – a drunken ass or a police plant embedded to divert attention before the storm came – it should have on some level signaled what was underway. It should have. But the lot of Occupiers and reporters who were still around – more than 50 of us – were approaching delirious. Most of us wouldn't have expected a raid if Lieutenant John Pike walked through waving a fistful of pepper spray.

And then it came. Right before 5am. Nobody really believed that it was coming. Even though we all knew that it was, and even though there couldn't have been a better opportunity for authorities to gain pole position over vulnerable campers. By the time Occupiers started yelling 'mic check,' the whole park was surrounded by cops – most in all-black action (but not riot) gear, others in sweet late-80's style waterproof reflective numbers. It's hard to remember what happened immediately after that. I blasted out some tweets and ran for a safe spot.

As I think everyone expected, Boston police were relatively respectful. The situation that transpired early this morning was unfortunate and even disgusting – at least in this reporter's eyes – but cops were not out to hurt or harm anything other than a whole lot of freedom of expression. From what I saw and experienced, those who did not wish to get bagged were given the opportunity to avoid arrest. That's only right, but considering the barbarism we've seen deployed against Occupy camps elsewhere I'm happy to show appreciation.

All that said, I did have a shitty encounter with some officers. After flashing my *Boston Phoenix* business card and embroidered company jacket, I was allowed into Dewey Square along with photographers and some other writers while police were mauling the camp. But after firing off a few tweets and snapping some pics, I felt a light tug at my backpack, and was told that I had to leave unless I could produce a proper press pass (which the Commonwealth of Massachusetts hasn't issued in a decade). In eight years of reporting at City Hall, the State House, police headquarters, and just about everywhere else in this city, I've never needed one. Until today.

My own eviction came just as cops started wrapping zip-ties around wrists. Not just on home base, but across Atlantic Avenue near South Station. That's where I was told to go unless I wanted to get locked. So I did. And there I found about 50 more Occupiers and other shunned press, plus more cops than I could count. That's not an exaggeration – it really seemed like they were multiplying, especially as they crossed Summer Street and held the line close to the sidewalk. People were told that they'd be arrested if they walked into the street. And some did, and were cuffed something fierce before being stuffed into wagons.

As is sort of being said by television news reporters, there was quite a bit of excitement on the South Station side of things. Some Occupiers made logistical announcements about meeting later at the Boston Common bandstand; others screamed at cops who remained more or less silent. After a few hours of this rigmarole, it's reported that just under 50 activists and approximately no white collar criminals were arrested.

Writing this dispatch back in my apartment, I'm having a good laugh at the morning coverage of events that I just lived through. To Channel 7, Mayor Tom Menino is the hero, even though he wasn't there. They also compared what happened this morning to playoff victory riots, and announced that, in just a few years, we might see the first Occupy presidential candidate. I'm not sure where that theory came from, but it sure as hell wasn't from the crowd that I was standing with on Summer Street. They're not thinking about a few years from now. They're thinking about where they'll be in a few hours.

December 06 | Day 81

Occupy Our Homes
Finally putting people
In vacant houses

December 07 | Day 82

San Fran reclaims park
Hurt protesters left to bleed
Ends on civil note

December 08 | Day 83

Judge rejects Boston
Raid could come any minute
Yet party ensues

December 09 | Day 84

Tension in Boston
Imminent camp ouster looms
Big tents broken down

December 10 | Day 85

Dewey evicted
End of encampment era
Longest-running done

December 11 | Day 86

West Coast announcement
Port shutdowns coming Monday
Hit rich in wallet

December 12 | Day 87

Occupy the Ports
Houston solidarity
Landlocked Boise too

December 13 | Day 88

McKeldin Square cleared
Peaceful but disappointing
Crowd hits City Hall

December 14 | Day 89

Time to face charges
Manhattan court occupied
Brooklyn Bridge backlash

December 15 | Day 90

Occupy Boehner
Speaker gets a golden calf
Biblically served

OCCUPY EVERYWHERE

Originally published in:
The Boston Phoenix, December 14, 2011

I don't know many people who were irreparably broken over the demise of Dewey. That goes for reporters and Occupiers alike, and even for many of the homeless folks who relied on camp for food, friends, and shelter. Like activists out West who were relieved to lose the burden of tent city albatrosses and the crimes that they attracted, Dewey refugees immediately saw positives in their eviction. I was personally saddened by the raid; it kind of felt like losing a lover for who I'd dropped everything. But if Occupiers suffered similar setbacks, most didn't show it. Instead they rallied in flocks from the moment they were booted. Looking back, it's obvious that Dewey was a drain. Still it took lots of gall for activists to keep trucking.

Forget the plowed debris field left at Dewey Square. That space is no longer synonymous with Occupy Boston – the movement is pushing forward. On Saturday evening – just hours after a 5am police raid cleared Dewey's tent city – Occupiers braved the cold to regroup at the Boston Common bandstand. On Sunday, they met there again to get down to business, planning a new strategy: Occupy Everywhere.

Already, neighborhood Occupy outposts are popping up from Allston to the suburbs. In Boston this week, more than a dozen well-attended working groups met each day. Without the burden of maintaining the campsite, the focus has been on action, and lots of it.

"Now a lot of stuff is behind us – stuff like planning for police raids," says Robin Jacks, an Occupier who has been chronicling the movement via Twitter since late September. "I'm not sad," she adds. "It was just like closing a door and opening a new one. Every working group is doing direct actions now. I've been to a million meetings so far, and I have about a million more to go to in the next few days."

There is still some unfinished business from Dewey – whatever else Occupy was, it was a home to people who now need new accommodations – but the passion and resolve of Occupiers is intact. The initial post-raid general assembly on the Common showed little of the academic grandstanding of past GAs, and talk of outreach and inclusion wasn't just intellectual masturbation. On Sunday, speakers announced key partnerships with critical community groups, from labor organizations like the Service Employees International Union, to the Jamaica Plain–based grassroots advocacy group City Life. According to Jacks: "As a group we've wanted to do this kind of outreach, but all the shit that came with Dewey was a distraction."

Some speakers expressed concern about "moving too fast from decompression to action." But the prevalent sentiment came from Marisa Egerstrom, a Harvard PhD candidate who's known by Occupiers as the Protest Chaplain.

In a tweet that was echoed widely, Egerstrom declared, "First we were a camp. And we needed that. That experience taught us how to become a movement."

REACHING OUT
The next challenge for Occupy Boston is to see if it can play well with others. At a Monday working-group meeting held at the SEIU offices downtown, Occupiers discussed the campaign with City Life. The tandem effort will officially begin this Friday, when Occupiers plan to join the organization's seasoned picketers in moving a woman and her family back into their Dorchester home. On Saturday, they'll proceed – together – with more "re-occupations," as well as other actions in solidarity with the Occupy Our Homes initiative, which has prompted similar collaborations nationwide. On Monday, Occupy and City Life will double-team Government Center to protest cuts to the US Department of Housing and Urban Development (HUD).

The two groups didn't always get along, and months ago such a partnership would have been far-fetched. At the first Occupy Boston general assemblies in September, reps from MassUniting – a federation representing hundreds of local advocacy groups, including City Life – asked for Occupy support in their September 30 sit-in at the Bank of America building on Federal Street. The offensive had been planned months in advance, with more than 50 actions leading up to the big day. But the nascent Occupy activists mostly ignored the call for collaboration, even voting to take Dewey on the same afternoon.

Wounds between Occupy and community groups didn't heal overnight. Despite a handful of Dewey Square protesters showing up at City Life foreclosure actions – and a successful Occupy the Hood event in October, in which hundreds marched from downtown to Roxbury – most relationships between the Occupy movement and other organizations have been superficial until now. Some groups viewed Occupy as a "rent-a-mob," while many Occupiers were skeptical of co-optation by unions and political action committees. There are still concerns – Tuesday's general assembly spent two hours weighing a proposal as to whether Occupy Boston should officially condemn Republicans and Democrats – but the worst of the paranoia seems to have faded.

Said Curdina Hill, executive director of City Life: "The MassUniting coalition will continue to stand on the front lines with Occupy Boston in the fight for a government and economy that works for all of us – not just major corporations and the wealthiest one percent."

At the Monday outreach meeting, Occupy coordinator Katie Gradowski explains to her comrades that it's important to respect City Life's leadership on upcoming anti-foreclosure actions. She says the nonprofit is excited about Occupy involvement, but needs to know exactly how they plan to help wage war against evictions. Will they bring flash mobs? Marching bands? Another Occupier adds that Occupy shouldn't compromise City Life by staging independent home occupations that could antagonize the police in already volatile neighborhoods.

Many working groups are attempting to unite ebony and Occupy. Significant outreach into minority communities has been a problem in the Boston movement since day one, but is now being steadfastly addressed. The people-of-color working group is forming a council of elders to court older black and minority activists who have experience engineering mass movements.

They already tapped veteran Hub hero Mel King to help the effort. To mesh with activists in the Latino community, Occupy offshoot Ocupemos El Barrio is asking for "white allies" to join them at a re-organizing meeting in East Boston this Friday. Some are even reaching out to adversaries. Media working group point person Martin (he doesn't give his last name) is planning a January town hall powwow at the Old South Meeting House to engage politicians and opponents of the movement.

"If they really want to listen to us, then they should come," Martin says about everyone from Republican pols to conservative trolls. "And if they want to work with us – and talk to us – they can wait at the podium like everyone else and have their say. . . . There are a lot of organizations on the outside and different kinds of people who are really helping, and those are the ones that we want to work with. The end result is to have everybody's input on what we should be doing moving forward."

LEFT BEHIND
Even with the open road ahead, Occupiers won't leave Dewey behind altogether. Many ex-campers marched from there to City Hall on Monday to protest their eviction, and are attempting to immortalize the space by bronzing the Gandhi statue that once watched over their encampment, leaving him permanently perched in the square as a memorial. Then there are the legal leftovers. Accused con man Paul "Fetch" Carnes is suing nearly a dozen Occupiers. Diehard protester Gary Williams faces criminal charges stemming from the now-infamous December 1 sink incident (a/k/a Sinkgate), when he allegedly assaulted a police officer by clinging to a steel tub that cops wouldn't allow in. There's also tension since Suffolk County District Attorney Dan Conley charged multiple men – who were arrested during last weekend's raid – with resisting arrest.

But it's not all heavy baggage. Jay Kelly, keeper of the Occupy Boston sign tent, has safely stowed flags and placards from their first days at camp, with hopes to show them in a gallery soon. Should Occupiers ever set up another camp, and for any outdoor actions in the future, the logistics team has an apartment packed with everything from warm blankets to bins filled with tampons. The medic squad also has its own stash of supplies, while the food operation continues to collect donations and feed evening assemblies.

"Right now, our goal is to take the graciously donated goods and figure out how to get them to the people they were intended for," says logistics hand Jennie Seidewand. "And then we need to figure out how to continue supporting and providing for not just our movement, but our communities, too."

They also have some money left. The Occupy Boston General Fund has more than $55,000, with another $10,000 coming that was raised for legal defense. Then there's roughly $4000 in a Greenway Fund – originally earmarked for repairs to Dewey Square, it's now in limbo – plus more than $2000 in cash boxes.

There's still a lot up in the air. Until Occupiers find a permanent indoor spot, they have accepted an invitation to have assemblies at the Cathedral Church of St. Paul on Tremont Street three times a week. In considering meeting and storage places, big questions include whether such facilities should have kitchen utilities and sleeping quarters. Right now, some Occupiers, having lost the only home they had at Dewey Square, are living with friends from camp. Others have returned to sometimes-dangerous shelters, leaving some working groups scrambling to find them safer spaces. It's a logistical nightmare to secure warm beds for one and all. But after everything they've been through, Occupiers finally seem ready to tackle such tasks without losing focus on the larger fight against economic injustice.

"There are people in the movement who are chronically homeless, and I don't have an answer for that," says Gunner Scott, a backbone of the media working group and a de facto Occupy Boston chief since the beginning. Scott says that it's important for the movement to secure a physical home base, where everyone from folks without computers to working stiffs with full-time jobs can rally.

Adds Brandon, another one-name Occupier and Food Not Bombs operative: "Even though we lost our physical space, the services that we provide have survived. Despite not having a space to organize out of, we're already focused on more things than before because we're not distracted by so many inner dramas. Not to downplay those dramas – especially considering what happened with the eviction – but there's a process here, and now it's a lot easier to follow."

OCCUPY THE FUTURE

Originally published in:
The Boston Phoenix, December 18, 2011

This chapter is a hybrid of two pieces: a blow-by-blow blog dispatch from December 17 anniversary actions at Occupy Wall Street (in which I chronicled a failed attempt to occupy Duarte Square), and a more formal account of those events that ran in the paper. In both, I also addressed two major Occupy-related conferences that were held in Manhattan that weekend – one at Pace University, and another much snootier summit at the New School. At the time, I wasn't very harsh about the absurdity of holding dueling movement conferences on the same day. In retrospect, though, I should have been more of an asshole, because it really is the perfect metaphor for both the ego trips and communication quagmires that have undermined Occupy all along.

After barreling straight ahead for more than three months, Occupy is at its first fundamental turning point.

Encampments in city after city have been eviscerated and plowed under. In Boston, after a judge ruled that the Dewey Square Occupation wasn't protected as free speech, protesters – with the help of police – broke camp and dispersed. All this while critics say the movement has to either take a new form or perish.

But in fact, Occupy has been moving toward that new form for months. Since early October, hundreds of activists from Occupations nationwide have been building connections by phone, e-mail, and Internet relay chats. Now, despite lower public visibility, this network is metamorphosing into something stronger and more sustainable – approaching what renowned group dynamics guru Clay Shirky calls "movement nirvana."

The biggest question now is what form the mature revolution will take. Not everyone agrees on whether to prioritize direct action or longitudinal strategy. This split played out over the weekend of Occupy Wall Street's three-month anniversary: on December 17, several hundred protesters rallied from lower Manhattan to midtown, and nearly 50 people were arrested for trying to set up a new camp. The following day, with much less media fanfare, more than 500 activists also met at two separate conferences in New York to map out the future of Occupy. In one of those summits – a symposium at the New School titled "Occupy Onwards" – Yotam Marom of OWS's direct-action working group attempted to strike a balance between the two sides.

"We can't expect to be in the headlines every day," said Marom. "So far, we punctured the narrative – that this is how things are, that there is no alternative, that people in America don't fight back, and that if you want to protest you have to get a permit. But we've just broken a crack in it, and we're just now getting to see what's on the other side."

D17

At the noon start time there are hardly more than 100 folks milling around Duarte Square, an obscure triangular slice of real estate on the northwest corner of Canal Street and Sixth Avenue in Manhattan. It's a certifiable Occupy event, complete with street theater, balloon metaphors, and an impromptu curbside teach-in on the evolution of the American police state. But for all the Web hype and build up to the third anniversary of Occupy Wall Street's taking of Zuccotti Park – dramatically hash-tagged #D17 it seems uneventful, so I grab Issue 5 of the *Occupied Wall Street Journal* and steal a bench down the block.

When I return 20 minutes later, the scene's changed dramatically. The painted and bandana-clad badasses are here – medics, direct action organizers, soldiers with helmets, gas masks, and a number of hard steel containers lutched onto their knapsacks with carabiners. Small swarms of other activists also arrive, including rally staples like Santa Claus, a Bradley Manning tribute teepee, and a drum circle grooving to the tune of someone chanting "Impeach Obama." By 1pm you'd need a helicopter to count the number of heads on the ground, especially if you're including cops, who are trolling the surrounding blocks and park perimeter.

The celebration and chatter goes on for nearly three hours before anything pops. But as 3pm approaches, people begin whispering instructions to prep for action. Soon enough hundreds start marching, punching north on Sixth with a caravan of scooter-mounted cops keeping the crowd packed on the sidewalk. More than ever before I realize how bad relations are between authorities and Wall Street Occupiers, as a torrent of insults fly in both directions, with some protesters calling cops "fat bastards," and police taunting right back. Among more than a dozen occupied cities that I've visited, New York activists are easily the most relentless in their verbal badgering of officers.

What first seems like a chaotic march with no clear purpose turns out to be a clever ruse. Occupiers had been eyeballing a vacant lot – beside Duarte – that was enclosed in ten-foot chain-link fencing, so a core team smuggles a towering step ladder in the middle of the pack. After a loud and distracting stroll around the block they get back to the lot, the ladder goes up, and brave protesters begin climbing over the fence – medics, direct action heroes, and retired Episcopal Bishop George Packard, who winds up being one of about 50 people arrested when cops rush in minutes later. It's a dangerous scene, and a sure sign of what's to come in the next few weeks.

That's all by 4pm, and Wall Street Occupiers are just getting started. From there they clock some more headlines, splitting up and stomping uptown in packs. One crew makes its way toward the home of a Trinity Church rector; the institution owns the land beside Duarte that they wished to Occupy, and Trinity – a former Occupy ally – told them to keep out of the abandoned yard. Further north, a second posse climbs all the way to Times Square, where they scramble the early evening shopping rush and sing "Happy Birthday" to Bradley Manning. By the end of the day, they'd made a spectacle for millions to see, and had a pic go viral of a bishop in a purple robe being handcuffed.

I traveled here to see first-hand how much gas is left in the mothership's tank. Occupy Wall Street – while populated by far more condescending and righteously bohemian soapbox salespeople than any other Occupy – is still the backbone of it all, and the energy level in New York affects the movement at large. While there's plenty of post-Dewey excitement at home, it's yet to be seen what kind of rally numbers Occupy Boston will be able to pull a month after losing its camp. But if places like Manhattan,

Oakland, and Portland are any indication, they'll be just fine in terms of people power and raw gusto.

INTEROCCUPY

While Marom and a number of core contributors have been strategizing from Occupy's Manhattan headquarters, activists elsewhere also started planning early on for the future. Joan Donovan is one of them. In October, Donovan, a Los Angeles–based sociologist, began participating in national conference calls that were first orchestrated by the Occupy Wall Street communications team, and that are now planned daily by her and others who coordinate interoccupy.org.

Within weeks of its inception, InterOccupy had hundreds of participants, many of whom wished to connect with not just other Occupations, but with people from specific working groups in distant places. Now, three months into Occupy, there are regularly scheduled cross-continental calls between food workers, general-assembly facilitators, and direct-action organizers, among others – the latter of whom Donovan says orchestrated the recent West Coast port shutdowns over a series of calls that lasted up to five hours apiece.

"The way the network works," says Donovan, "is that nodes are fairly independent of one another. It's like the way ginger grows. If you take off a knuckle in one place, and re-plant it somewhere else, it will grow back strong. The movement is experiencing this in a rapid form. You have these Occupations that work independently of each other, but we rely on each Occupation recognizing the ethic of the movement – that we are nonviolent, and that we are targeting the one percent."

Shirky, the group-dynamics expert who also authored the ever-relevant organizing guide *Here Comes Everybody*, recently met with Donovan and other "meta-movement builders" at Pace

University, where he explained how networks like InterOccupy can help larger efforts thrive. At this point, according to Shirky, Occupy is fast-evolving into "loosely connected clusters of tightly connected clusters."

As Occupy grows, says Shirky, good ideas will inevitably flourish, while bad ones will flame out – just as they have at individual camps.

LEVEL NEXT

Occupy wasn't started by people interested in caution. And while there's a seemingly ubiquitous notion that the movement needs organization, many are pressing forward with a series of high-profile direct actions. Next week, swarms of activists in Iowa have pledged to disrupt the Republican caucuses as best they can. The same goes for Occupiers in New Hampshire, who have their own plan for spoiling the coming primaries. There are also major efforts under way in DC, where activists from all over will descend on the Washington Mall on January 17, plus aggressive actions planned for both national political party conventions, and an all-out Midwestern onslaught slated for May, when the G8 and NATO summits are both scheduled to be held in Chicago.

In the meantime, individual Occupy movements have to sustain themselves. To that end, Occupiers in cities like New York and Chicago have rented spaces to hold working-group meetings, while activists in those and other places are considering more full-service facilities where allies can also eat and sleep. Marianne Manilov, a consultant with the Oakland-based Engage Network who works closely with the movement, says such local hubs are critical.

"It's unbelievably important to have a place to meet, and to greet, and to eat with each other," says Manilov. "It's more than just socializing – it's about connecting with the people who you're fighting with."

Along those lines, there's a permeating attitude that the immediate next phase of Occupy should proceed at a slower, more calculated pace. At the recent "Occupy Onwards" conference, human-rights crusader L.A. Kauffman of the Global Justice Movement said adjustments are necessary if Occupy stands a chance of being more than just another line on the resume of career activists.

"It's very easy when involved in direct action to find yourself chasing the high," said Kauffman. "That experience can become addictive, and it can be tempting to continue doing the same thing. . . . It's a tricky moment, but simply following the urge to keep acting right now is not the wisest thing for Occupy Wall Street to do. They should take advantage of the seasonal imperative and hunker down to strategize."

In that statement Kauffman didn't get much disagreement from Occupy Wall Street direct-action group member Marom. Still determined to score regular wins on issues like student and worker rights – quick highs for the common good that will keep Occupy awake and expanding – Marom nonetheless concedes that the worst thing at this point would be for people to burn out.

"In the first two months, you had to be out there all the time, and it was a total adrenaline rush," said Kauffman. "You don't sleep, you don't eat – you don't want the movement to die. But the reality is that it's going to take at least a decade to have a meaningful social transformation. And if that's going to happen, then the next bunch of years can't look the same as the first two months. . . . Sometimes you have to go and see your mother. She's been calling."

December 16 | Day 91

Congress hunger strike
Rep Ellison starves a day
Backs DC protests

December 17 | Day 92

Three months already
New York swarms Duarte Square
Party and arrests

December 18 | Day 93

Pace U conference
Upstaged by New School summit
Dueling protest meets

December 19 | Day 94

Occupy Caucus
Iowa direct action
Against Obama

December 20 | Day 95

Cop war escalates
Anons post private info
Cue the subpoenas

December 21 | Day 96

Berkeley squatters warned
This can't go on forever
Camp getting sketchy

December 22 | Day 97

Drama in the Bay
Berkeley tents plowed asunder
Welcome to the club

December 23 | Day 98

City of LA
Plans to sue Occupiers
Bankers still okay

December 24 | Day 99

AP announces
Folks hoarding Occupy kitsch
Making history

December 25 | Day 100

Occupy Christmas
Ninety-ninth night has arrived
Not merry for all

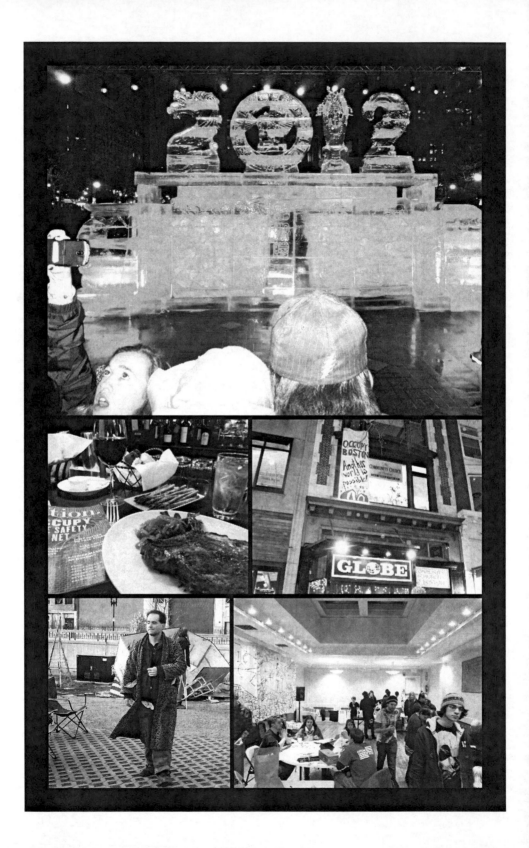

OCCUPY THE NEW YEAR

Originally published in:
The Boston Phoenix, January 1, 2012

An hour before linking up with Occupy revelers on December 31, I puffed a blunt thicker than a porterhouse and grubbed a bone-in ribeye with a chalice of Malbec at Grill 23. In between bites, sips, and reading *The Nation*, I jotted notes about how I might end my book. When I began this project, I planned to manufacture closure – hence the whole 99 nights gimmick, which refers to the exact number of days between September 17, the birthdate of Occupy Wall Street, and Christmas, the birthdate of Jesus Christ. In light of how the movement evolved, though, and my experience with Dewey ex-pats on New Year's Eve, I didn't have to fudge a finale after all. In some form or another, Occupy will continue on for decades. But that doesn't mean there can't be happy endings along the way.

If the Boston Police Department had undercover officers embedded in the Occupy Boston First Night operation, they would have found a whole mess of juicy goods to bring back to the Suffolk County district attorney's office. From the baking of free cookies to the holding of signs, prosecutors could have implicated a number of activists in unspecified crimes against no one in particular.

Days before Christmas, news broke that the DA had subpoenaed Twitter hashtags and handles linked to the movement. Occupiers await results on that front, as documents remain sealed from a private hearing with a Suffolk judge last Thursday. But while the ACLU fought in court to protect the First Amendment rights of those slapped by the subpoena, local activists persevered, and on Saturday organized a First Night barrage that revealed the sort of tomfoolery that might be making authorities nervous.

The Tiny Tent Task Force was on the prowl, armed with little paper tents made of cardboard and cancelled credit cards. Strategically situating their metaphoric miniatures around Boston, the squad used their creations as conversation starters with potential sympathizers. It was a brave move for the team of artists, whose chessboard-size encampment outside of Bank of America's Boston headquarters last week prompted a BPD intervention that played out like *Gulliver's Travels* in both scale and allegory.

At the Community Church of Boston above Copley Square – a congregation point for various progressive causes, so an obvious choice of headquarters for Occupy First Night operations – the movement's local Screen Print Guild got stamping. In the final hours of 2011, they committed countless acts of free speech on T-shirts and bandanas.

Outside, partygoers hung a story-high banner: ANOTHER WORLD IS POSSIBLE. Beneath that sign, at around 8pm, dozens of former Dewey Square regulars stood on the sidewalk and across Boylston Street waiting for the Occupy Boston Women's Caucus to shine its "bat signal." Before long, messages of hope and solidarity – plus their enduring "We Are the 99 Percent" mantra – projected over Copley, while activists cheered and chanted with some unsuspecting First Night–goers joining in.

Authorities could have found any number of suspicious activities underway – the peace vigil could have been easily mistaken for a satanic séance, and who knows what was in those holiday brownies? Still, the Occupy New Year's scene in the Hub was far from what transpired in Manhattan, where more than 60 were arrested trying to reclaim Zuccotti Park. Occupy Wall Street's Boston counterparts went for a decidedly different kind of spectacle, planning weeks ahead of time to make a positive first impression on visiting suburban crowds.

There was collateral payoff to their jovial approach. In the middle of it all, something happened that summed up the attitude that many Occupy Boston folks say they hope to embrace – in some form or another – in 2012. Frank Tosney, who famously helped run the food tent in a Flinstonian fur coat at the Dewey camp, was hanging at the Community Church, when a young Occupier approached him. "I just want to apologize for any shit that might have gone down back at camp," the kid said. "Don't even worry about it," Tosney told him. "All that stuff is behind us now."

PARTY CRASHERS

Originally published in:
The Boston Phoenix, January 11, 2012

Before Occupy was a glimmer in an activist's eye, the New Hampshire primary was the most exciting thing I'd ever covered. In 2004, I got to witness ridiculous spectacles like Wesley Clark's campaign, and Howard Dean's flame-out in the face of John Kerry's mediocrity. The depravity continued four years later, as both major parties were busy slumming in the Granite State. Still those experiences hardly compare to 2012, as this time Occupiers – joined on the front lines by hostile Ron Paul supporters – offered the closest thing to a significant third party presence that New Hampshire's ever seen. In the end, Occupy's Primary victories were largely ignored in most media coverage. But that doesn't mean their voices weren't heard. Anyone who claims that is full of more shit than Mitt Romney at an all-you-can-eat press conference.

The nation's first presidential primary isn't new terrain for activists. From anti-Vietnam crusades in 1968, to collegiate battalions fighting nukes in the '80s, to Bush bashers eight years ago – protesters have rocked the Granite State as much as the frigid weather there has permitted. So it's of no surprise to anyone – other than right-wing talkers who've declared them dead and irrelevant – that hundreds of Occupiers flocked to the state that could pick their next oppressor. Considering the oddly warm recent temperatures, it was a no-brainer.

In the weeks leading up to New Hampshire, activists had connected through conference calls and social media, pooling resources in order to amplify their message at the quadrennial circus. Once on the ground, by Friday Occupiers from as far as Washington, DC, and even Las Vegas had transformed Veterans Memorial Park – smack in the heart of downtown Manchester – into a full-service operation, complete with tents for everything from media to medical. From there, they got to relentlessly bird-dogging candidates and riling conservatives all the way through an encore flash mob on Tuesday afternoon.

"This has been my dream for years," says perennial presidential candidate Vermin Supreme. An anarchist godfather in these parts, Supreme says the primary's been an increasingly popular protest destination, but at times also a "clusterfuck" of different causes. Occupy, he says, puts a number of those forces in the same tent. "I've been trying to get people to occupy the primary for years, and this is bigger and better than I've ever seen it. The movement's caught up with my vision. . . . I'm surging in spilling Santorum."

SHOTS FIRED
Though the first official Occupy the Primary general assembly isn't for days, the onslaught pops off less than 12 hours after the Iowa caucus results come in. With Ron Paul taking a much-

needed rest, and Rick Santorum greasing South Carolina voters, the obvious target is Mitt Romney, who's speaking at Manchester Central High School with his new friend and sidekick, Senator John McCain.

Like a starter pistol for primary protesters, Manchester native and Occupy soldier Mark Provost – announcing himself as part of the movement – asks the first question after Romney wraps up his half-hour of war-mongering and China-bashing. Long-winded and hollow-tipped, the inquiry – impugning Romney's controversial statements about corporate personhood – rattles the candidate, who'd been otherwise composed.

Responding to Provost, Romney assumes his patronizing CEO persona with a speech on the birds and bees of job creation. He's shook having to answer a peasant, but a follow-up question on health care proves easier to tee-off on; Romney realizes that the woman's reading from a script, and knocks her off balance before ramming his stump down her throat. The Occupiers aren't done, though, and Provost continues interrupting out of turn until McCain scolds him like an old man who finds his grandson in his dildo drawer.

HORSEMEN OF THE A-PAUL-COLYPSE

It's a frenzy outside of the second primary-week debate, this one hosted by NBC's *Meet the Press* at the Capitol Center for the Arts in Concord. To the right of the theater, Occupiers gather for a wedding ceremony – officiated by none other than Vermin Supreme, decked in tattered Uncle Sam attire – between a woman in a flowing white dress and a man wearing a Bank of America effigy. "Who can screw me harder than this corporation?" says the bride, Occupy activist Elizabeth Ropp from Manchester.

There are others who stand out: Bill Higgins and Judy Hammond of Dover, who brought their pet goat Izak to attract eyeballs to their Jon Huntsman sign; Hasidic Jews railing against Zionism; a gaggle of laborers shilling for some guy named Obama. But in what's being marked as one of the quietest primary seasons in recent memory as far as native participation, there's no doubt that the loudest folks in town represent either Ron Paul or Occupy – two factions that, while there's some common ground between them, are beginning to really loathe each other. I'm not sure when the beef started, but the tension's been palpable since three Paul supporters swung through the Occupy camp on Saturday – on horseback – waving Tea Party flags.

By the end of the debate, Paul fans and Occupiers are battling for pole position by the door. The latter group, now more than 50 strong, directs as much spite toward Paul's posse as they do the exiting candidates. Occupiers chant: "We want transparency. We want honesty." The loudest screamer for Paul responds: "Then you should be with us!" To which one Occupier barks: "Ron Paul is a disgusting pig and fuck you!"

NEWT AND THE BOOT
Occupiers aren't banging on the windows of Don Quijote Restaurant, where Newt Gingrich is holding his Latino outreach party. It just sounds that way, as Provost – who fired the first shot at Romney days before – is smashing on a drum outside, trolling the restaurant's perimeter. Along with him are about 25 Occupiers nailing different tasks: an undercover team of two scatters anti-Newt signs in the bar area; one woman, holding an "Occupy Hartford" sign and hollering, is physically removed by security; Vermin – boot on his head and bullhorn in hand – sticks his placard inside the rear window until a Gingrich goon forces his arm out and slams the pane.

The scene escalates as Gingrich enters to Toby Keith's "Made in America." Screams and snares seep through the doors and vents, and the candidate stumbles on talking points related to everything from energy policy to how Michael Bloomberg bought his mayorship. By the time he launches into his "this is truly a land of opportunity" spiel, virtually all members of the press are choking on laughter, trying to glimpse the provocateurs who are penetrating from beyond the wall, telling Gingrich that he's an alien and instructing him to come out with his arms up.

FROTHY PICKET

There's a pathetic dad at Rick Santorum's final meet-and-greet before the polls open. With his pre-teen son watching, the turkey-necked dolt physically reaches across the bar at Jillian's for Santorum – "RICK!!!" – only to be ignored completely. Humiliated, he tries to salvage his manhood by attacking the Paul backers and Occupiers who are sniffing at the windows of Jillian's: "Do you see those people outside?" he says. "They're mad at you and me because they don't have jobs."

But they do have a job. Tonight, it's to crash Santorum's party, which they're doing by filling the windows with accusatory signs, and creeping around every corner. The candidate walks through, but is then rushed into a back room so that all the windows can be covered in campaign banners before he tells everyone how "America as we know it will be gone." if the president wins re-election. Occupiers had already spoiled his event at a diner on the east side of Manchester days earlier. The campaign staff wasn't about to let it happen again – especially after word got around that Occupiers had just forced Gingrich to cancel an event by bombarding his Manchester headquarters.

Santorum is rushed into the parking lot, where a mad horde of Paul people and Occupiers form a scrum to get at him. As the candidate exits the bar, a chorus chants "Frothy bigot!" Candidate Supreme reaches in to shake Santorum's hand, but is pushed away by campaign staffers. It's the most aggressive brush of the week, as two of Vermin's own staffers are shoved to the ground. For the first time since the debate in Concord, the Paul crew and their Occupy nemeses agree on something to chant in unison: "Shame!"

BATTLING SCIENTOLOGY

Originally published in:
The Boston Phoenix, October 23, 2008

Before I wrote enough on Occupy to fill a whole encyclopedia, my initial plan was to include this age-old opus as a bonus to fill space. Still for the purpose of explaining the viral outbreak at the root of the movement, my piece on the Web activist outfit Anonymous – and its war on the Church of Scientology – is as integral as any story that I've written since. Though it was my first *Boston Phoenix* cover piece (and by far the longest article I'd published up to that point), I still stand firmly behind "Battling Scientology." If my work reporting on foreclosures and oppressed people braced me to cover Occupy out in the streets, then my time spent tracking Anonymous and Gregg Housh – who went on to be a major player in both Dewey and Zuccotti – prepared me to navigate the online ecosystem that makes the movement tick.

In a world wracked with uncertainty, there is at least one thing you can bet on: pick a fight with the Church of Scientology (CoS), and its leaders will fight back – always with vigor, often with a vengeance, and sometimes with litigation that can be long and costly.

The idea of locking legal horns with the CoS might be enough to cool the ardor of some critics. But that is not Gregg Housh's style. Housh, an Internet activist and provocateur, is not an easy guy to characterize. A member of a group that calls itself "Anonymous," Housh is pitted in what appears to be an escalating rift with the CoS. Core constitutional issues such as freedom of speech and freedom of religion are central to the dispute.

Almost 10 months ago, Housh helped launch a protest group that he now describes as the world's fastest-growing grassroots movement (mobilizing several thousand people in less than one month). The group formed as a response to the removal of a video from YouTube and other sites that featured Tom Cruise describing CoS doctrines and principles. From a few simple mouse clicks, a mighty battle has grown.

Housh is himself a rather casual, almost random sort of activist. A seventh-grade dropout, devout atheist, and proud computer troll, he claims to loathe all political parties equally, and could give a damn about Greenpeace, PETA, or any other picket-happy causes. In fact, had the CoS not "messed" with what he thinks of as his Internets, Housh would probably be wasting his spare time sparking Web mischief instead of dedicating approximately 40 hours every week to Anonymous, his now infamously masked group, whose mission seems to be toying with L. Ron Hubbard's minions.

Born in Dallas in 1976, Housh deserted middle school to pursue technological endeavors. He's been a hacker, a programmer, and a hardware technician, leaving one city for another every time he got bored and found an attractive new job offer. In 2002, he moved from the Florida Keys to Boston for a gig in financial analytics, but quit after finding cubicle life to be impossibly tedious. He still lives in the Boston area and still works with computers (his current job is one of two things he won't discuss, the other being the three months he served in federal prison for copyright infringement via software piracy), but Housh is hardly blinging off the commonwealth's supposed tech boom. On January 21 – the day he and four other Anonymous members (or Anons, as they call themselves) posted their "Message to Scientology" video on YouTube – he reports having had just $144 in the bank. Less than one year later, he describes his account as negative-$1400 and plummeting.

Since the CoS successfully pursued criminal complaints against him this past March, Housh has endured 10 pre-trial dates for charges including harassment and disturbing the peace. You might think a guy who's inundated with litigation would step off, or, at least, avoid exacerbating his legal predicament and feud with the well-endowed CoS by spilling to any and all inquiring reporters. But Housh is like Cool Hand Luke (without the chiseled abs), a quixotic figure who, perhaps against his better judgment, has refused to back down. The first time the *Phoenix* contacted him for this profile, he stated, quite seriously: "The more they come at me, the more I'm going right back at these fuckers."

DISTURBING THE SPEECH?
Today, on October 11, Housh can't join his associates to rally outside the CoS's Boston property for the ninth Anonymous protest in nine months – due to a restraining order set by the Boston Municipal Court, he's forbidden to walk within 100 yards of the church building at 448 Beacon Street. But that doesn't stop

him from participating: at 11:30am, he emerges from the Hynes Convention Center MBTA stop with a dozen other Anons, most of whom are dressed as zombies in what they say is homage to CoS members who either died under questionable circumstances or committed suicide. The jovially raucous group parades down Newbury Street, then hangs a left down Hereford Street chanting "Scientology kills," effectively shattering Back Bay's tree-lined tranquility and gaining the attention of any and all passers-by.

After Housh makes plans to reunite with the group later near Boston University, his accomplices join about 30 other Anons who are already outside the CoS building wielding literature and signs. These costumed pranksters have a singular goal, which, according to an October 4 Anonymous press release, is to expose "the illegal and immoral behavior of the Church of Scientology." Their oak tags read: "Ron Is Gone But the Con Lives On," "Honk If You Oppose Scientology," and various slogans alleging that the CoS shatters families and financially fleeces its members.

Taking cues from boom boxes on two corners at the intersection of Hereford and Beacon, the Anons dance hysterically to their anthem, "Tom Cruise Crazy," plus Haddaway's "What Is Love?", Rick Astley's "Together Forever," and several other songs that were recorded when most of these late teens and twentysomethings were wearing Pampers. If anything, their antics are silly; the police officers on duty see no need for alarm – one appears to doze off, while the other thumbs a newspaper. Through the ordeal, CoS members, who in the past have openly taped and photographed protesters, utterly ignore the scene, cordially entering and exiting the church in small groups as if there weren't 40 young adults mocking them and shouting insults. Passing pedestrians and motorists, however, pay attention: maybe two out of every 10 drivers heed one sign that reads, "Honk If You Oppose Destructive Cults."

For students from the nearby optometry school, as well as most other observers snapping cell-phone pics and chuckling, the compelling visual attraction is the fact that many of these Anonymous members are wearing Guy Fawkes masks inspired by the film *V for Vendetta*. But while the masks were first intended to conceal their identities and protect against CoS retaliation, Anonymous's signature accessory might be its legal undoing. Church authorities already know the identities of at least six other local Anons (and hundreds nationwide), and have threatened legal action against past and future protest activity. The CoS argues that masks – combined with the group's aggressive behavior – constitute criminal harassment: "Anonymous seems to have the mistaken impression that mask wearing is a protected form of free speech," says Boston CoS attorney Marc LaCasse. "Mask wearing, in fact, is not speech – it is conduct . . . it is disturbing religious worship, and it is disturbing the peace."

Still, Housh and other devout operatives soldier on by consistently turning out at monthly protests in front of Scientology churches across the planet. (The next is scheduled to take place internationally this weekend on Saturday, October 18; Boston Anonymous held its monthly event this past weekend instead, as its members will be busy this weekend handing out flyers at the Head of the Charles Regatta.) Alex Vanino – an outed New York Anon and anti-CoS Web honcho who drove up this past Saturday from Westchester despite having received a cease-and-desist notice from the CoS – isn't scared. "There's nothing they can do to get us," says Vanino, adding that he is motivated by his friend who he claims committed suicide after Scientology indoctrinated him to stop taking anti-psychotic medication. "I've done a lot of research on this, and everything we're doing here is clearly legal."

UNLIKELY CRUSADER

Housh is clean-cut but not preppy – a scrawny, baby-faced jeans-and-sneakers kind of dude whose appearance doesn't advertise his interests. That said, he's not socially or aesthetically rugged whatsoever. Housh doesn't so much as drink booze or get high – soda pop and controversy-fueled adrenaline are his intoxicants of choice. Though he has the credentials and demeanor of a stereotypical circuit head, Housh claims that's not the case. "I'm not one of those basement dwellers," he says. "I've had a wife and all of that – I even go out to clubs and do stuff."

One year ago, Housh never would have thought that even semi-extroverted computer types like him could mobilize in the flesh, as thousands have since done at rallies that Anonymous says span more than 100 cities in 40-plus countries. Nor did he have reason to. He and other regular visitors to gleefully raunchy image boards such as 711chan.org and 4chan.org had pulled several stunts – such as the "Great Habbo Hotel Raid of '06," in which users bombarded the virtual social-networking site Habbo with thousands of Don King–styled avatars – but they were hardly prone to public tomfoolery. Until recently, most pedestrian Web surfers had no idea what Housh, or any of the other trolls who instigate Internet pranks and post degenerate pictures on 4chan, were up to.

"I've been on 4chan for years, and it's not a Web site you would ever want to send your mom to," says Housh. "Originally, it forced people to log in anonymously, which is where the name 'Anonymous' comes from. One of the goals of threads on there is simply to scare people away – it's always been one of those places that you go when you're bored and you just want something really vulgar to entertain you."

Housh's 4chan frolicking took a dramatic turn on January 14, after Hollywood investigative journalist Mark Ebner posted a video of Tom Cruise touting Scientology's virtues on YouTube. Presumably embarrassed by the leaked footage – in which Cruise claims that believers are the only people who are capable of helping car-crash victims – CoS attorneys, citing to intellectual property rights and the Digital Millennium Copyright Act (DMCA), pressed YouTube to remove the clip just hours after it was posted. As quickly as YouTube yanked it, 4chan and Internet Relay Chat (IRC) channels spewed forth assertions that the DMCA was being abused. At least three rebels re-posted the video on YouTube. Those postings, too, were removed almost immediately.

Housh seems to view himself and his cohorts as Web-savvy Paul Reveres, sounding the alarm about encroaching Internet transgressions. "Originally, this was about 'You don't do that on our Internets,'" says Housh. "They need to understand that, and these are the lessons they learn when they piss people off. You have to play nice – they did not have the right to pull that." As Wendy Seltzer, a fellow at the Berkman Center for Internet & Society at Harvard Law School, explained to the *Phoenix*, the removal was not warranted, since the CoS can't quantitatively prove that the leak affected any specific Scientology product's market value. As of now, it can be found on YouTube.

FROM THE WEB TO THE REAL WORLD
Housh and his Anonymous peers are hardly the first to fight the CoS online. The original anti-Scientology Web site, the newsgroup alt.religion.scientology, debuted on Usenet in July 1991. For its first three years, the site actually served as a forum for believers and dissenters to exchange opinions, but by 1994 users on the Scientology side had had enough. A memo written by CoS staffer Elaine Siegel addressed church strategy vis-à-vis dealing with dissenters on the Web. "If you imagine 40 to 50 Scientologists posting on the Internet every few days, we'll just run the SPs [Suppressive Persons] right off the system. It will be quite simple

. . . I would like to hear from you on your ideas to make the Internet a safe space for Scientology to expand into." Her memo seemed to enrage secular alt.religion.scientology regulars.

The CoS did more than just post pro-Scientology messages where opposition surfaced. In 1995, it turned to the justice system, claiming that its copyrighted files were being illegally posted on alt.religion.scientology. The dispute over such materials, which parishioners pay tens or even hundreds of thousands of dollars to obtain on their journey – or "bridge" – to enlightenment, has been the centerpiece of most CoS feuds with Web detractors. That year, the FBI raided several Usenet posters' homes, including that of former Scientologist Arnaldo Lerma in Arlington, Virginia, seizing his computer and data-storage devices.

The CoS has a well-documented history of battling opponents: Boston attorney Michael Flynn, who filed lawsuits through the 1980s on behalf of former CoS devotees, was sued more than a dozen times. Reporters, who CoS founder Hubbard labeled "merchants of chaos," have also been targeted; former *Time* magazine journalist Richard Behar, whose 1991 exposé "The Thriving Cult of Greed and Power" provoked widespread anti-CoS sentiment, found himself under surveillance by CoS investigators while his magazine was sued for $416 million. (The suit was ultimately dismissed, but only after Time Warner Inc. spent $7 million defending itself.) But whereas individuals and even corporations were relatively easy to tie up in lawsuits, the Web posed a newer, less containable wave of protest. In a December 1995 *Wired* article titled "alt.scientology.war," writer Wendy M. Grossman described the rift as "mortal combat between two alien cultures. . . . A fight that has burst the banks of the Net and into the real world of police, lawyers, and armed search and seizure." (The CoS declined to comment on copyright-related litigation.) CoS actions to quiet online enemies have provoked a great deal of anger. According to Seltzer, contrarian sites such as xenu.net have proliferated as a result. Launched in 1996 by Norwegian tech-provocateur Andreas Heldal-Lund, xenu.net – a comprehensive anti-CoS clearing-house better known as Operation Clambake – became a hub for multimedia, ranging from articles condemning Scientology to detailed insider accounts written by former church officials and secret Hubbard recordings. The church has sued, among others, Heldal-Lund, his service provider, and Google over Operation Clambake postings. It has succeeded in having various copyrighted materials removed. Yet xenu.net remains alive and clicking. Xenu, by the way, is a reference to an evil intergalactic overlord who, top church members reportedly believe, excommunicated billions of aliens to Earth 75 million years ago and incinerated them inside volcanoes. The title, Operation Clambake, is a poke at the late Hubbard's claim, from his 1952 book, *Scientology: A History of Man*, that humans evolved from clams.

A MOVEMENT IS BORN
Housh and his pajama army took up the Operation Clambake cause with vigor. They saw the CoS as fighting dirty – both online and off. Housh and his colleagues figured they could fight back, even if they were mostly Web heads who had never met each other, or, for that matter, participated in protests that required them to leave the house. Within hours of CoS attorneys' forcing YouTube to remove the first few Tom Cruise videos on January 15, Housh estimates that 20 to 30 instigators began uploading the clip on hundreds, if not thousands, of Web sites. An anonymous 4chan post the following day suggested that people unite on a common Internet Relay Chat (IRC) channel and declare war against Scientology. Project Chanology, Anonymous's anti-CoS initiative, was born.

There was, however, a lack of organization. So on January 17, Housh and four other Anons broke off into a separate channel that they specifically created to discuss press strategies. "A few people were saying that there should be a press release," says Housh. "There were five of us at that point, and one guy said he was a writer, one was a proofreader, and I had some good ideas for structure. We started pounding it out, and by the end it looked more like a video script than a press release. Then the other two guys said they were into video and had the tools, and one of them said they had some creepy cloud footage. The next thing you know, we have 'Message to Scientology' up on YouTube on the 21st."

The "Message to Scientology" video, two minutes in length, has been played several million times between YouTube and a number of other host sites, including Gawker. In it, an eerie synthesized voice declares: "Hello, Leaders of Scientology. We are Anonymous. Over the years, we have been watching you. Your campaigns of misinformation, suppression of dissent, your litigious nature: all of these things have caught our eye. With the leakage of your latest propaganda video into mainstream circulation, the extent of your malign influence over those who have come to trust you as leaders has been made clear to us. Anonymous has therefore decided that your organization should be destroyed."

At first the message of the video – which also promised "We do not forgive. We do not forget. Expect us." – was mostly bark inspired by tough talk that Housh and his comrades likely internalized from sci-fi antagonists. But then legions followed suit. Though Housh contends that he did not participate in the ensuing cyber raids, which the CoS calls "cyber-terrorism," or in the bomb threats that Boston CoS members allegedly received, he giggles when discussing how CoS-related sites were terrorized in the days after "Message" was posted.

"People started going into channels and saying, 'Take this tool, go to this site, and run it,' " remembers Housh of the potentially dangerous computer viruses that circulated through 4chan. "That's really stupid . . . because you don't know what kind of virus was in there, but the people creating these tools were not designing them to hurt us – they were designed to hurt them. There wasn't real skill being used other than by a few people who showed up with real DDS [Distributed Denial of Service] capabilities – the masses were mostly just killing bandwidth – slowing sites down and making them die every now and then."

With "Message to Scientology" drawing YouTube hits in the millions, the IRC channel that birthed the movement consequently had a flood of new arrivals who were eager to enlist with Project Chanology. When the heavy traffic made it difficult for people to engage in dialogue, one member of Housh's ad-lib press corps suggested that Anons break off into channels according to their hometowns. "It was doable because just knowing what city someone is in doesn't mean they have to give up their identity," he says. "People could remain anonymous."

With users separated into dozens of geographic groups by locale – including London, Boston, Tokyo, and Southern California – one member of the original press group (who has remained anonymous) reportedly realized that there was potential to take the project to another level if they could mobilize manpower off line. "We were just screwing with the Scientologists because it was fun to screw with them," says Housh. "But one guy was saying that, if we actually did something and the organization really went somewhere, then we've changed the face of activism on this planet for good."

On January 27, Housh and his cronies posted "Call to Action" on YouTube. The video picked up where "Message" finished, declaring: "Anonymous is not simply a group of super hackers. Anonymous is a collective of individuals united by an awareness that someone must do the right thing. . . . Among our numbers you will find individuals from all walks of life – lawyers, parents,

IT professionals, members of law enforcement, college students . . . and more. . . . We have no leaders . . . Anonymous invites you to join us in an act of solidarity. . . . Join us in protest outside of Scientology centers worldwide." The announcement called for folks to rally on February 10 – the birthday of Lisa McPherson, a Scientologist who Anonymous alleges, and the CoS denies, died in December 1995 because church officials blocked her from receiving adequate medical and psychiatric treatment.

With plans to protest at the Beacon Street CoS the next morning, Housh says he began receiving word on the evening of February 9 that Anons were already showing up in other cities. "First there were six people in New Zealand," he recalls. "Then Sydney, Australia, happened, and there were 250 people there. Then Perth, Adelaide, and Melbourne – they all had over 100 people – we broke 1000 before we left Australia. There was even one guy in Tokyo with balls of steel who went and picketed by himself. I love that guy."

When Housh finally met up in Back Bay with other local Anons, throngs of protesters were already outside churches in Hamburg, Berlin, Tel-Aviv, and London. In Boston, Housh filed a protest permit with the transportation department for 100–125 people – by day's end, he claims, there were about 280 masked Anons. (For events held since April in Boston, that number has thinned to a steady 40 or 50. Anonymous claims that, across the globe, approximately 10,000 people participated in the first, February 10 event. CoS attorney LaCasse claims those numbers are inflated.) Making good on the "Message" pledge to fight long and hard, Housh courted to keep the Anon community for future events. "At the first protest, we were handing out flyers for the next one, so that way, when everybody went home, they knew it wasn't done," says Housh. "You can't lose them for a second – we needed to keep everyone's attention."

ANONYMOUS NO LONGER

Certainly Housh managed to get the Scientologists' attention. On March 1, he joined some other Anons to distribute flyers throughout Boston. At around noon, his masked team approached the Beacon Street CoS, where they walked through the front door and, according to Housh, non-threateningly hand-delivered literature to parishioners. LaCasse and church member Gerard Renna viewed things very differently. Nine days later, they filed an application for a criminal complaint with the Boston Police Department claiming, according to the report, that Housh and "nine followers entered the Church of Scientology and disrupted church services by alarming the church members who were there to worship." Renna and LaCasse, who obtained Housh's identity from the February 10 protest permit, also told police they would seek criminal complaints in the Boston Municipal Court – a promise they kept on March 12. Three days later, Housh still joined Anonymous for its second planned protest, at which people ate cake and wore paper hats to mock Hubbard's March 13 birthday.

Initially, two complaints – trespassing and criminal harassment – were filed against Housh in what *Massachusetts Lawyers Weekly* described as "an unusual case pitting First Amendment free-speech protections against an individual's right to practice religion without harassment." CoS complainants presented the Suffolk County District Attorney with evidence that labeled Anonymous as a terrorist group, and alleged that members crossed the line between free speech and harassment by hiding their faces.

To Housh's attorney, Elizabeth Duffy, his conduct was "plainly within the First Amendment protections." LaCasse counters: "They make noise, they play loud music, and they encourage passing motorists to honk their horns by holding up signs that say 'Honk If You Hate Scientology.' This week was Yom Kippur – what do you think the reaction would have been if Gregg Housh took a sign that said 'Honk If You Hate Jews' and stood in front of a synagogue in Brookline? It is not just protesting. It is not free speech. It is criminal conduct."

Housh is not the only Anon to face Scientology's litigation tactics. A Los Angeles protester named Sean Carasov spent 10 hours behind bars and more than $5000 fighting charges that stemmed from CoS complaints – he further claims that someone from the church near his East Hollywood home poisoned his cat. Unlike Housh, Carasov has no idea how he was outed.

Having had legitimate organizational experience in the real-life work force as a record-industry veteran who has worked closely with the Clash and the Beastie Boys, Carasov took an unofficial leadership role with the SoCal Anons early on. In addition to the monthly protests, he and another since-outed dissident named Gareth Alan Cales orchestrated "mini raids" just to remind the CoS that they were still out there. One such incident took place on March 11, but without Cales there to tame him, Carasov – a self-described "ex-soccer hooligan who likes a punch up every now and then" – heaved a torrent of insults at camcorder-wielding Scientologists. Two days later, the CoS posted the video (ironically on YouTube) exposing his identity. Four days later, at the second official Anonymous protest, he was arrested for making felony criminal threats for his actions of March 11. The charges were ultimately dropped for lack of evidence, but for reasons including, as he contends, his fear of covert CoS tactics, Carasov has since hung up his mask.

"This fucking thing punched a big hole in my life," says Carasov. "We all knew they were crazy, but we didn't think they could get away with this shit. I almost have a grudging respect – it's part of the game. We fucked with them, and they fucked me in the ass. Plus, they only recruit rich people into the church anyway, and I fucking hate rich people. If they're stupid enough to go there in the first place, then why should I help them?"

Housh reacts differently, even though the CoS has (admittedly) sent investigators to follow him, and even though his legal woes have no end in sight. Between rallies, he helps maintain whyweprotest.net – a dynamic hub for all things Anonymous that boasts a 400,000-person e-mail list – and consults for other anti-CoS sites, including exscientologykids.com, which is operated by three church defectors, including Jenna Miscavige Hill, the niece of Scientology leader David Miscavige. In September, two new charges were brought against Housh – for disturbing the peace and disturbing religious worship. So far, the case has passed through the hands of four different Boston Municipal Court judges, with three charges remaining intact.

While Anonymous has no formal hierarchy, it appears that, when it comes to issues involving the CoS in Boston, Housh is a key organizer; still, renegade Anons didn't have to consult with Housh (and didn't) about picketing Katie Holmes's Broadway debut earlier this month in New York (in previews, and they planned to protest Opening Night this week), or hacking Sarah Palin's e-mail this past month, or "raiding" various Web sites with whom they have a beef, such as allhiphop.com in June.

Still, while there are no sanctioned leaders, Anonymous has advanced an uncompromising strike against Scientology.

"None of us had any clue about how to do any of this before," says Housh, "and now people are starting to recognize us. We were handing out flyers on Boylston Street recently and this one guy walked right past us, so I yelled, 'Sir – at least tell us that you're with us.' When he realized that we were against Scientology, he turned around, told us to turn on our cameras, stuck both middle fingers in the air, and yelled, 'Hey, Tom Cruise – fuck you!'"

CREDITS

WORDS

Chris Faraone

DESIGN

Alfredo C. Rico-Dimas

PICS

Daniel Callahan
Chris Faraone
Derek Kouyoumjian
Paul Quitoriano
Ariel Shearer

EDITS

Carly Carioli
Shaula Clark
Peter Kadzis
Sean Kerrigan
S.I. Rosenbaum

ACKNOWLEDGEMENTS

This project would have sucked if not for a lot of people, but extra special thanks to the following:

Writers, Occupiers, & Freedom Fighters Everywhere

Mom & Tony
Dad & Anne

Matt & the Abramson Clan
Grandma & the Albanese Clan
Chris & the Bellapianta Clan
Danielle & the Bello Clan
Michael & the Belmonte Clan
The Biddy Early's Clan
Ryan & the Delaney Clan
The Faraone Clan
Reed & the Fuller Clan
Knife & the Good Life Clan
Trees, Marty, & the JTTS Clan
Dan & the McCarthy Clan
Dan & the McCluskey Clan
Stephen, Brad, & the Mindich Clan
Max, Cheyenne, & the Quinn Clan
Caleb & the Rogers Clan
Kerry & the Ronan Clan
Gaetano & the Tarara Clan
The UNregular Clan
Alex & the Urevick Clan
The Verso Clan
The Walsh Clan
Erik & the Wallin Clan
Spencer & the Walter Clan
Greg & the Williamson Clan
Ghostface & the Wu-Tang Clan

and most of all...
My *Boston Phoenix* Family